DATE DUE

~~2-31~~-04			
6-23-12			

Demco No. 62-0549

Set design by John Lee Beatty
Photo by Carol Rosegg

A scene from the Guthrie Theater production of *To Fool the Eye*.

TO FOOL THE EYE
AN ADAPTATION OF JEAN ANOUILH'S *LÉOCADIA*

BY JEFFREY HATCHER

DRAMATISTS
PLAY SERVICE
INC.

TO FOOL THE EYE
Adaptation Copyright © 2000, Jeffrey Hatcher

Original French Version
Copyright © 1939, The Estate of Jean Anouilh

All Rights Reserved

CAUTION: Professionals and amateurs are hereby warned that performance of TO FOOL THE EYE is subject to payment of a royalty. It is fully protected under the copyright laws of the United States of America, and of all countries covered by the International Copyright Union (including the Dominion of Canada and the rest of the British Commonwealth), and of all countries covered by the Pan-American Copyright Convention, the Universal Copyright Convention, the Berne Convention, and of all countries with which the United States has reciprocal copyright relations. All rights, including professional/amateur stage rights, motion picture, recitation, lecturing, public reading, radio broadcasting, television, video or sound recording, all other forms of mechanical or electronic reproduction, such as CD-ROM, CD-I, DVD, information storage and retrieval systems and photocopying, and the rights of translation into foreign languages, are strictly reserved. Particular emphasis is placed upon the matter of readings, permission for which must be secured from the Adapter's agent in writing.

The English language stock and amateur stage performance rights in the United States, its territories, possessions and Canada for TO FOOL THE EYE are controlled exclusively by DRAMATISTS PLAY SERVICE, INC., 440 Park Avenue South, New York, NY 10016. No professional or nonprofessional performance of the Play may be given without obtaining in advance the written permission of DRAMATISTS PLAY SERVICE, INC., and paying the requisite fee.

Inquiries concerning all other rights should be addressed to Abrams Artists Agency, 275 Seventh Avenue, 26th Floor, New York, NY 10001. Attn: Charmaine Ferenczi.

SPECIAL NOTE
Anyone receiving permission to produce TO FOOL THE EYE is required to give credit to the Author and Adapter as sole and exclusive Author and Adapter of the Play on the title page of all programs distributed in connection with performances of the Play and in all instances in which the title of the Play appears for purposes of advertising, publicizing or otherwise exploiting the Play and/or a production thereof. The names of the Author and Adapter must always appear in the same size and prominence on separate lines, in which no other names appear, immediately beneath the title and in size of type equal to 50% of the size of the largest, most prominent letter used for the title of the Play. No person, firm or entity may receive credit larger or more prominent than that accorded the Author and Adapter. The billing must appears as follows:

TO FOOL THE EYE
An Adaptation of Jean Anouilh's *Léocadia*
by Jeffrey Hatcher

The following acknowledgment must appear in all programs distributed in connection with performances of the Play in size of type less than 50% of the size of the largest, most prominent letter used for the title of the Play:

To Fool the Eye is based on a literal translation by Stephanie L. Debner.

In addition, the following acknowledgment must appear on the title page of all programs distributed in connection with performances of the Play:

This adaptation was originally commissioned and produced
by the Guthrie Theater, Joe Dowling, Artistic Director.

SPECIAL NOTE ON MUSIC
For productions electing to make use of the music to "Where Went the Waltz," included herein, the following acknowledgment must appear in all programs distributed in connection with performances of the Play:

"Where Went the Waltz"
Music by Andrew Cooke
Lyrics by Jeffrey Hatcher

for John Miller-Stephany

TO FOOL THE EYE was produced by the Guthrie Theater (Joe Dowling, Artistic Director; David Hawkanson, Managing Director) in Minneapolis, Minnesota, on October 7, 2000. It was directed by John Miller-Stephany; the set design was by John Lee Beatty; the lighting design was by Kenneth Posner; the sound design was by Scott W. Edwards; the composer/musical director was Andrew Cooke; the costume design was by Mathew J. LeFebvre; the dramaturgy was by Michael Lupu; the voice and text coach was Robert Neff Williams; the movement coach was Marcela Lorca; the assistant director was Katherine I. Murphy; the production stage manager was Russell W. Johnson; and the assistant stage manager was Chris A. Code. The cast was as follows:

AMANDA	Melinda Page Hamilton
DUCHESS	Barbara Bryne
BUTLER	Steven Epp
HECTOR	Denis Holmes
TAXI DRIVER	Kris L. Nelson
ICE-CREAM VENDOR	Dudley Riggs
PRINCE ALBERT	Scott Ferrara
HEADWAITER	Jim Lichtscheidl
BELA, A GYPSY/VALET	Joey Babay
MARIA, A GYPSY	Molly Sue McDonald
NIKOS, A GYPSY	Richard Long
FLAGEL, A GYPSY/VALET	Michael Kissin
PESHKE, A GYPSY/VALET	Peter Vitale
HUNTING AIDE	Mark Rosenwinkel
INN PROPRIETOR/VALET	Dan Foss

AUTHOR'S NOTE

The first page or so of *To Fool the Eye* is taken up with a lengthy bit of schtick.

In Jean Anouilh's *Léocadia*, upon which this adaptation is based, the play begins with the character of Amanda waiting in a luxurious room dominated by a statue. When Guthrie director John Miller-Stephany and I sat down to discuss what this statue might look like in our production, we came upon the idea that perhaps the statue was one of those cherubs often found as part of a small fountain. A cherub with openings in every orifice, through which water could spout. This lead to further thoughts — all of them comic. We decided the first scene would be set in a solarium, thus allowing for a small indoor fountain. Our clever and resourceful designer John Lee Beatty assured us such a fountain with full running water could be built and made functional on the Guthrie stage, so I wrote the fountain — and the fountain schtick — into the script.

The schtick remains, but I grant some theaters might choose to start the play with less grand aquatic activity. If so, simply delete the fountain and its attendant schtick. You'll still need the statue for various plot reasons, so keep the figure, but skip the water. As Jean Anouilh would probably attest, the play worked just fine in Paris without it.

—Jeffrey Hatcher

CAST SIZE

The Guthrie production of *To Fool the Eye* had a cast of seven men, two women, *plus* a "Gypsy Band," made up of four performers, each of whom played an instrument and sang. That brings the cast size to thirteen (the Guthrie could afford it). I can imagine less extravagant budgeting that allows for fewer performers. By doubling the actors who play the Ice-Cream Vendor, the Taxi Driver, the Butler and the Inn Proprietor with the "Gypsy Band" (lots of droopy black mustaches), not only can you save money, but you'll give four funny actors more to do. Do they have to be able to play instruments? No. It can be recorded and faked onstage (fakery being a theme of the play). But make sure you use Andrew Cooke's music and employ the standard gypsy instruments: accordion, violin, guitar and tambourine. Anything else just isn't gypsy.

CHARACTERS

AMANDA
DUCHESS
BUTLER
HECTOR
TAXI DRIVER
ICE-CREAM VENDOR
PRINCE ALBERT
HEADWAITER
INN PROPRIETOR
MARIA
NIKOS
FLAGEL
PESHKE
VALETS

TIME

Early to mid-1930s.

TO FOOL THE EYE

ACT ONE

Scene 1

A room of overwhelming luxury. For our purposes let's call it a solarium. The time period is the early to mid-1930s, but the house is from another century entirely.

There's lots of tile and wrought iron and glass. Plants all around. Ticking clocks. A small porcelain stove. Most important: a statue. A cherubic pissoir sort of thing, perched in the middle of a tiny, indoor fountain. There's water in the tiny fountain, but no water coming out of the little fellow's stone penis.

At rise, Amanda is seated in one of the wrought-iron chairs, a small cardboard suitcase at her feet. She seems to have been sitting here for a long time. She's quite pretty. Young. Intelligent. Her attire suggests a working-class woman who has donned her best travelling clothes for an important interview. She wears green gloves.

Amanda sighs. She looks around the solarium. Her eye is caught by the cherub pissoir statue. After a moment, she rises and moves to the statue. She gazes at the little figure. Her eyes travel down to his not-so-little penis. She stares at it. She reaches out to it — tentatively. She lightly touches a valve or button and suddenly a stream of water comes out of it and into the fountain.

Amanda jumps back from the now shooting stream. After a few moments, the stream stops.

Amanda looks offstage to see if anyone saw what she did — at which point another shot of water shoots out of the penis. Amanda looks back at the statue. The stream stops. She looks away again. A shot of water shoots out. She looks back at the statue. It stops. She stares at it a long time.

Amanda slowly looks away again, keeping her eye on the statue to the very last. Once she's looked fully away, she glances back at the statue, as if to "catch" it.

It doesn't spurt. She looks away again and then darts another glance back at it. No spurt.

Amanda smiles, satisfied, and turns fully away — at which point the water shoots out of the penis again. Followed by water shooting out of the cherub's bottom, mouth, nose and ears. Water is shooting out of every possible orifice.

Amanda panics and runs around the statue, as if trying to find a way to stem the tide or find its secret button — all to no avail.

As the water burbles on, Amanda senses someone approaching. She dashes back to her seat and tries to resume a pose of calm, innocent serenity.

A slight woman enters, preceded by her very long lorgnette. It is the Duchess. She goes to the statue, slaps its bottom, and the water stops running. Then she turns to Amanda and beams at her through her lorgnette.

DUCHESS. Is it really who I think it is? Or do my eyes deceive?
AMANDA. No, Madame — I mean, oui, Madame, I'm … I mean, I think I'm who you think I am. I think.
DUCHESS. Lift your head. *(Amanda does so.)* Higher. *(Amanda*

lifts it higher still.) Higher. *(Ditto.)* Look up. *(Looks up.)* Look down. *(Looks down.)* Look left. *(Looks left.)* Look right. *(Looks right.)* Left. Right. Left. Right. Left, right, left, right — *(Amanda follows orders.)* — right. *(Amanda looks left.)* Ha! Tricked you! Stand up. *(Amanda stands.)* Straighter. *(Amanda straightens. Duchess surveys her coolly.)* Why is it you aren't taller?
AMANDA. I don't know, Madame. I try my best.
DUCHESS. Try harder. *(Looks at Amanda's feet.)* I see you're wearing shoes.
AMANDA. … Er…?
DUCHESS. I too wear shoes. I am sixty years old and have never worn anything but Louis XV.
AMANDA. The king?
DUCHESS. The heels. How tall are you in stocking feet?
AMANDA. Five foot two.
DUCHESS. *(Vexed.)* In stocking feet I am five foot one. But since no one has ever seen me without shoes, consider yourself shorter. Naturally, my late husband, the duke, saw me without shoes. He saw me without shoes on more than one occasion, but as he was nearsighted and kept a proper distance, I doubt he knew the truth. *(Squints at Amanda's gloves.)* What are those?
AMANDA. *(A bit embarrassed.)* Gloves.
DUCHESS. They're going to the dogs.
AMANDA. To the — ?
DUCHESS. Just an expression. My dogs wouldn't accept them. I loathe the color green, and I fear my opinion has rubbed off on them. Now they're fairly militant about it. Well, they're poodles, they're particular. Not that they even know what the color green is, nothing here is green. The only thing green in this house … is your gloves. *(She throws them in the porcelain stove.)*
AMANDA. But, Madame, I paid quite a lot for those gloves!
DUCHESS. You were taken. *(Looks at Amanda's hand.)* Delicate hands, fine fingers. They've sewn their share of hats, but there's good lineage in them, somewhere, in the distant past. Not that I've anything against sewing hats. What woman in these days hasn't sewn a hat? Me, actually. Were you informed as to what you would be offered here this evening?
AMANDA. A job, I think, Madame.

DUCHESS. *(Exclaims.)* "A job!" What a quaint expression. The girl is precious. *(Stares deeply at Amanda.)* Am I not correct, Gaston? *(As they are alone in the room, Amanda looks around her.)* Gaston is the duke. He died in 1913, but I've never been able to break the habit of talking to him. *(Sits.)* So! Are you happy to have found a — what was the phrase? — "a job"?
AMANDA. Oh, oui, Madame! I can be frank with you because they gave me such good references; but the Reseda sisters who employed me until two days ago were forced, through no fault of mine, to let me go.
DUCHESS. *(Stands up and goes to the door.)* I know. It was I who forced them to.
AMANDA. *(Stands also, flustered.)* You? Well ... that's pretty ... pretty —
DUCHESS. Hm...?
AMANDA. ... Gutsy!
DUCHESS. *(Smiles, pleased.)* "Gutsy!" It sounds like a board game! Gaston, I told you she was precious, and she's just that: precious! *(The Duchess glides out of the room. Amanda sinks down to her chair. She is beginning to want to cry. A butler enters and bows before her.)*
BUTLER. Pardon me, Mademoiselle, but the duchess would like to inquire whether Mademoiselle would be interested in a light repast.
AMANDA. I'm not hungry.
BUTLER. That wasn't a question, Mademoiselle. My voice did not go up at the end of my sentence. The duchess has ordered me to serve Mademoiselle this repast whether Mademoiselle wants it or not. *(An extraordinary snack is served by valets with an unashamed show of silver. Amanda is presented with a table stacked with too many cakes and too many fruit dishes. Finally she timidly takes a tangerine and begins to peel it. The Duchess enters in a gust of wind, followed by Hector, an old country squire who looks like he smells a bit ripe. She goes to Amanda, snatches the tangerine from her and throws it in the stove.)*
DUCHESS. Who brought this fruit? I do not want lemons, I do not want oranges, and I most particularly do not want mangoes! You eat fruit, you lose weight, and you, my pet, cannot afford to lose an ounce. Wouldn't she be stunning, Hector, if she had a hint more heft? *(Hector, who has put on his monocle to look at Amanda, doesn't have time to respond.)* Eggs!

AMANDA. Pardon, Madame?
DUCHESS. Theophilus! *(The Butler enters immediately.)*
BUTLER. Madame?
DUCHESS. Remove this eruption of citrus and bring forth some eggs! Lots and lots of eggs!
BUTLER. Oui, Madame.
AMANDA. *(Rises, resolute.)* No!
DUCHESS. *(Turns back, surprised.)* "No"? I don't think I've ever heard that word. Mademoiselle, what means this "no"?
AMANDA. I'm not hungry. And I never eat eggs.
DUCHESS. *(To Hector.)* Precious.
HECTOR. *(Echoing.)* Precious. *(Duchess and Hector exit.)*
BUTLER. Citrus begone! *(Valets take away the food. Amanda tries to get the attention of the valets.)*
AMANDA. Are … are they coming back? Excuse me. Are … are they…? Will someone tell me why I have been brought here?
BUTLER. Mademoiselle must forgive, but none of the staff is privy to what I think you would call "information." If Mademoiselle wants that, might I suggest to her that it will be necessary to speak directly to either the duchess or, in lieu of her presence, to Baron Hector, the deferential and somewhat overripe gentleman who follows in her wake. *(The Butler exits. Amanda, remaining alone, hurls her suitcase to the ground and angrily stamps her foot.)*
AMANDA. Ohhhhhh! Shinny, shinny, shinny! *(Duchess reenters.)*
DUCHESS. Oh my, an expletive. "Shinny," a middle-class genteel derivation of the word "shit." Dear girl, a word to the wise: if one intends "shit," one must say "shit." Shinny is simply shit without the guts. I know you must be dying to see your room and rest up after your long journey, but there is someone due to return to this house very shortly and it is imperative he not see you.
AMANDA. Madame, this morning I received a telegram, in your name, offering employment. Is it fair to assume you take me for a fool?
DUCHESS. My dear, I take what I can get.
AMANDA. I should've guessed. Why would a rich woman like you want to hire a woman who makes hats?
DUCHESS. True, rich as the rich are, we seldom hire live-in hat-makers.

13

AMANDA. I will tell you this: if the job you're offering is that of a maid or a companion, the answer is no. I have a profession already!
DUCHESS. She is a child, Gaston, but she has qualities — attributes — *(Lances at her like a fencing master.)* — reflexes. *(Duchess starts to exit again.)*
AMANDA. *(Jumping in front of her.)* Oh, no you don't! You're not leaving this room!
DUCHESS. Gaston! We are prisoners in our own home! The child intends to hold us hostage just like François the First!
AMANDA. François the First?
DUCHESS. Who once sentenced our ancestors to house arrest, and though the house is large and filled with amusements they bored themselves to death.
AMANDA. I am not holding you hostage! Madame, I came here on the two-sixteen train, it is now almost five o'clock, the last train back to Paris is at five-thirty-nine and I am going to be on it!
DUCHESS. Actually, no, you won't.
AMANDA. Why not?
DUCHESS. The five-thirty-nine has been cancelled.
AMANDA. … You did it, didn't you? You had the five-thirty-nine cancelled so I couldn't leave this house!
DUCHESS. My dear, it was not I who cancelled your train. It was the unions. You see, in these stringent times, I have taken to allowing tours of the estate chapel. It's been quite a boon to us, and, I can tell you, the devotees of Karl Marx don't like it one bit. Once they realized the trains were permitting people to visit here, all of a sudden, bang! No more 5:39! But I'm not beaten yet. I'm planning to smuggle tourists in on buses disguised as nuns. Nuns trump Karl Marx any day. *(The Duchess starts to leave. Amanda's voice stops her.)*
AMANDA. Madame, I don't know about chapels and unions and nuns. All I know is that I've been waiting here for more than two hours; I didn't even have breakfast this morning before I left.
DUCHESS. Why do you think I ordered you the eggs! A diet of eggs is guaranteed to increase your bustline without adding weight! Don't believe me. Believe the Viennese doctor I paid ten thousand francs to tell me that! Now where are those eggs…? *(She goes to leave again. Amanda emits a wail.)*
AMANDA. Oh! No, Madame! No, don't leave again! OH! I'm

going crazy in here!
DUCHESS. *(Stops, returns, then solemnly.)* Dear girl. I have a confession to make. I am not sixty. I am sixty-seven. In my lifetime, I have seen the rise of the Impressionists, the invention of hairpins, the death of Franz Ferdinand and the growing popularity of blue cheese. And if I've been going in and out of here like a Swiss Miss on a cuckoo clock, I have my reasons. But I'm not telling! Not yet! *(The Duchess zips off again. Amanda watches her go, then snatches up her suitcase.)*
AMANDA. That's it! That's the last they've seen of me! Aristocratic lunatics! I'll go back to Paris on foot! *(Amanda exits. The stage remains empty for a second; the Duchess and Hector rush back in.)*
DUCHESS. Hector! ... Hector! ... Where is she, Hector? Where is she? Oh, Hector, I am seized by a frightful premonition.
HECTOR. You've a right to, my dear. The bird has flown the coop!
DUCHESS. But Hector, if she meets him in the garden ... it will spoil the plot! *(They leave immediately. Blackout. Music up. It ends with the chirping of birds. When the light comes back, we are in a very rustic landscape.)*

Scene 2

A crossroads in the park of the chateau, a circular bench around a small obelisk. In a corner, stopped near a large tree, is an old-fashioned taxi. It is a funny taxi, faded, antiquated. It is surrounded by ivy and honeysuckle. Not far from there is the cart of an ice-cream vendor, candy pink and green. Under the taxi and the ice-cream cart — a pair of legs each. Amanda enters at a run with her suitcase. She stops, seeing the taxi, and emits a cry of joy.

AMANDA. Ohh! Thank heavens! A taxi! *(She discovers the legs.)* Monsieur!
ICE-CREAM VENDOR'S VOICE. Oui?

AMANDA. *(Confused.)* Er … Do these legs belong to you? *(The Ice-Cream Vendor comes out from within the cart. The taxi driver's legs don't move. He looks down at the legs.)*
ICE-CREAM VENDOR. No. But thanks for asking. *(Ice-Cream Vendor starts to go back to his business.)*
AMANDA. Monsieur, please! Can you tell me if I am still on the grounds of the chateau? I've been running and running for the longest time, and yet I never seem to get out!
ICE-CREAM VENDOR. You can run till you turn into butter, you'll still be on the grounds of the chateau. *(Amanda takes up her suitcase and runs to the taxi.)*
AMANDA. Ohhh … Taxi? TAXI?! Are you free? *(At these words, the Driver comes out furiously from underneath his car.)*
DRIVER. FREE? Of course I'm free! I'm French, I'm free, I'm a Free French Fellow! *(Amanda gets in the back of the taxi.)*
AMANDA. To the train station! Quickly! *(The Driver watches, deadpan. Amanda jumps out again.)* Driver?
DRIVER. Oui?
AMANDA. There are rabbits in your taxi.
DRIVER. *(Aching for a fight.)* You saying I don't have the right to raise rabbits?
AMANDA. It's not really a question of rights —
DRIVER. We fought a revolution for the right to raise rabbits!
AMANDA. Monsieur, I grant you have every right —
DRIVER. *(Sarcastic.)* Oh, you "grant" me my right! You GRANT me! I'm so LUCKY! I'm so BLESSED! Marie Antoinette here has given me a "thumbs-up" on rabbits!
AMANDA. I'm not Marie —
DRIVER. Let me tell you something, CITIZEN! I am a HUMAN BEING! Does not a human being have feelings? If you pinch him, does he not get a tiny welt on his arm? If you slap him, does he not say, "Hey, stop slappin' me!"?
AMANDA. *(Looks around.)* Is there anyone else here I can talk to?
DRIVER. I'm a worker! The day I got my first union card, I'd vowed I'd never be a lackey to the aristocracy! My union card said, "Automotive Transportation Engineer." Now that's a job title a man can take home to his mother! And now … *(Crumbles, whimpers.)* Now look at me! Bought and paid for at 3,000 francs a month!

Stripped of dignity and steeped in shame! Thank you, Mademoiselle! Thank you for coming by today to remind me how low I have sunk!
AMANDA. *(Who continues to step back.)* You're welcome. *(Backs into some vine.)* OH! What're all these weeds?
DRIVER. I wanted to grow roses, but it's hard to grow roses on this kind of axle and running board, so I went with weeds.
AMANDA. But how does your taxi run if it's covered in weeds?
DRIVER. People tell you you're funny, don't they? *(He goes to the engine, furious, gives it a turn of the crank, the engine turns over. He exults.)* HA!
AMANDA. How could I have doubted you? Do the weeds come with you when you drive?
DRIVER. "Drive?" Who said I drive?
AMANDA. Well, I assumed since you're a driver —
DRIVER. Assume nothing here, CITIZEN! I may be a driver, but I do not drive! The motor runs, but the meter does not!
AMANDA. *(To Ice-Cream Vendor.)* Monsieur, may I ask you a question?
ICE-CREAM VENDOR. Oui.
AMANDA. Are you really an ice-cream vendor?
ICE-CREAM VENDOR. Oui.
AMANDA. Do you sell ice cream?
ICE-CREAM VENDOR. No.
AMANDA. Did you EVER sell ice cream?
ICE-CREAM VENDOR. Oui.
AMANDA. But you do not sell ice cream?
ICE-CREAM VENDOR. No.
AMANDA. Thank you very much. I was afraid things were beginning to make sense.
ICE-CREAM VENDOR. Oh, rest assured, Mademoiselle, I do not make, sell or even recall the ingredients to ice cream. I believe it was cold, chunky and hard … but I may be confusing it with my wife.
AMANDA. *(Removes a hatpin.)* Here. Take this pin.
ICE-CREAM VENDOR. Why?
AMANDA. Prick me. Not too hard. Just enough so I'll know I'm not having a nightmare. *(He does indeed prick her.)* Ow!
ICE-CREAM VENDOR. *(To driver.)* Say, she's fun!

DRIVER. Says you! *(Ice-Cream Vendor pricks her again and again.)*
AMANDA. Ow! OUCH! HEY! *(Moves away.)*
ICE-CREAM VENDOR. Come back, we'll play pincushion!
AMANDA. *(Takes back pin.)* One needs the odd prick on occasion to remind us what's real. And to that end I am now going to walk straight in this direction until I find a road, a real road. And on this real road there will be a real sign. And I will read this real sign because I can really read. And I will walk with my two real legs to the real station and there I will find a stationmaster, and he too will be real and he'll have his very own real train. *(Picks up suitcase, close to tears.)* At least, I hope so. *(As she is going to leave, she runs into the Duchess who sweeps in like a whirlwind with Hector.)*
DUCHESS. *(Exultant.)* Heaven be praised, we've found her! *(Collapses.)* Smelling salts, Hector, smelling salts, lest I die of fright!
AMANDA. I'm the one who has reason to be frightened!
DUCHESS. You? Afraid? But of what, my dear?
AMANDA. That house! That taxi driver and his taxi covered with weeds! That ice-cream man who doesn't sell ice cream! YOU! Madame, what is it you want with me? I am a shopgirl from the Rue de la Paix; I never have adventures, I don't have money or a fiancée to pay my ransom! Please, I beg you, Madame, answer me: why did you have me fired from the hat shop and why have you lured me here with that fake job offer!
DUCHESS. Precious.
HECTOR. Precious. The very word. *(Amanda drops into her seat, at the end of her strength, near tears.)*
AMANDA. All I want is to get to the station …
DUCHESS. Oh, now don't cry! It has been proved beyond a shadow of a doubt that if I see someone cry I can't help crying and rolling on the ground.
HECTOR. And you don't want to see that.
AMANDA. *(Sniffles.)* I suppose not …
HECTOR. Even the poodles won't watch.
DUCHESS. There, I knew you'd see reason. You may be short, but you are sensitive to an old woman's grief. I have made a decision! I am going to put an end to the mystery, painful though it will be. Get ready. Sit up. All that was murky and muck is about to become clear as crystal. *(Inhales, slaps her cheeks, blows through*

her lips, sighs.) Mademoiselle … I have a nephew. *(Long pause.)*
AMANDA. And — ?
DUCHESS. Don't interrupt.
AMANDA. I thought you were finished.
DUCHESS. It was a dramatic pause.
AMANDA. Pardon me.
DUCHESS. I have a nephew … whom I adore more than anything in the world. His name is Albert. Albert, the Unfortunate. Albert, the Victim. Albert, the Melancholic. Albert, the Gloomy. Sad Albert, Albert Le Mope … Well, you grasp the concept. *(Turns away, on the verge of tears.)* Oh, Hector, you do it! The tale is too poignant. I doubt I have the will to tell it. *(Hector stands up ceremoniously. The Duchess presents him in a deadpan tone.)* Mademoiselle, my cousin Hector, the Baron Andinet of Andaine. *(Hector bows. He starts to speak, and the Duchess cuts him off.)* Not to be confused with Baron Jerome, attaché to the consulate of Honolulu; nor with Baron Jasmin, the son of Baron General Andinet. Baron Hector. Hector, go ahead. And now … Baron Hector. *(Hector bows again and is going to speak; the Duchess interrupts him.)* Not that you'd really confuse him with Baron Jasmin, since Baron Jasmin is dead, but I digress. Hector. Speak.
HECTOR. *(Purple tones.)* "The tale of the Prince Troubiscoi … "
DUCHESS. Footnote here. My younger sister became a Troubiscoi by her second marriage. The tsar was visiting and, well, Slavic charm being what it is, she wed the late prince, had a child and died. Continue, Hector.
HECTOR. *(Purple tones.)* "The tale of the Prince Troubiscoi … "
DUCHESS. A little insert here. Let's say, "Prince Albert," or "the Prince," or "Albert." Continue, Hector.
HECTOR. *(Purple tones.)* "The tale … "
DUCHESS. Hector, get to the point! It's really a good story, and he makes it sound so dull. Create some interest!
HECTOR. *(Deadpan.)* "Once upon a time — "
DUCHESS. Oh, forget it! Two years ago, my little Albert went to Dinard for a weekend and fell madly in love with a certain … "woman." A woman of great beauty, a woman so singular, so original that it was said they broke the mold once the cast of her was complete. A woman of whom I am sure even you have heard:

Léocadia Gardi.
AMANDA. Léocadia Gardi, the opera singer?
DUCHESS. The "Divine Gardi." Such a voice! In singing the prologue to *Astarte* she became notorious for the manner in which she sang: *(Sings.)* "Salut, Seigneur, sur cette terre … " *(Stops.)* That is not the manner in which *she* sang it, that is the manner in which *I* sing it, and I don't sing. I sang when I was young, but it was a little voice, like a whisper of sugar on a ray of sun until one day I drank too much ice water and froze my sugary wisp of a sunlight voice. Did you know Léocadia well?
AMANDA. I knew of her. I mean I read about it when she … died.
DUCHESS. And such a death it was. Léocadia Gardi was the kind of woman who wore scarves. The most immense scarves, the most passionate scarves, scarves that seemed to take on a life of their own. She had a special way of tying them, am I not right, Hector?
HECTOR. She tied a very passionate knot.
DUCHESS. One evening, after an interminable discussion of art, culture and the soul, she left some friends at the threshold of their improbably steep villa and tossed back her scarf in bidding "Adieu." Unfortunately, her gesture surpassed her neck and she was strangled. They say she emitted a cry …
HECTOR. A strangled cry.
DUCHESS. And then she fell, lifeless, breathless, songless … *(Overcome.)*
HECTOR. Dead.
DUCHESS. Dead! A mere three days after having met my little Albert who had completely and hopelessly fallen in love with her. When he learned the news Albert tried to throw himself off the balcony, but I pulled him back from the brink not once but many times. Luckily, coattails were worn long that season. Oh, but Albert was inconsolable. I tried to distract him by taking him on a cruise around the world one and a half times.
HECTOR. Which means when it's over you're very far away from home.
DUCHESS. We passed the full 122 days of that voyage, him in his cabin staring at her photograph, me watching him through the keyhole so that he didn't throw himself out the porthole. Shall I tell you about those 122 days, my dear? Shall I describe in detail

every whip and flail of my abject sea-tossed martyrdom?
AMANDA. No, that's —
DUCHESS. You're right, it's too depressing. But know you this: I, who am curiosity itself, made a trip and a half around the world with my nose inserted into a keyhole! Oh, sometimes I glanced out the porthole. I'd glimpse a turban, I'd say, "Well, that's India … " "Pigtail down the back of a neck, that's China … " "Two men kissing, welcome to Greece!" But then we returned home, and something odd started to happen to Albert. The first thing he did once we'd cleared customs was go straight to Dinard. So I had him followed by detectives. I learned he spent his days in the town, chatting sometimes with a taxi driver, sometimes with an ice-cream vendor. At night he went to a café with a gypsy theme, always the same table, always the same waiter. September came and Dinard emptied. But the gypsy café remained open, and Albert spent his nights there alone. Albert was paying the café to stay open for him!
HECTOR. And on the off-season!
DUCHESS. At first, it didn't make sense to me, but then, all of a sudden, it did. That café —
AMANDA. *(Affected by it all.)* … Was where they first fell in love!
DUCHESS. Hector, she may be a shopgirl, she may be part of the unwashed masses, but what took our brains so long to understand her heart grasps in an instant! You're right, my pet: the taxi driver, the ice-cream man, the café all were witness to his love for the "Divine Léocadia." Poor Albert!
AMANDA. How wonderful to love like that!
DUCHESS. Wonderful?! Albert is a Troubiscoi! An Andinet of Andaine! I'm not a reactionary fossil, but why should one's family bother to dominate half the continent of Europe since the reign of Louis the Sixth, if 700 years later one's nephew is allowed to run around with taxi drivers and ice-cream men? One might as well work! Still. I knew these taxi and ice-cream men were Albert's means of recapturing a beautiful memory, so I contacted each of them. I didn't know which was the most important touchstone for Albert, so I bought an assortment. Every person who'd come into contact with the couple during their three days of happiness was engaged by me to become part of the staff here. I bought the taxi, the ice-cream cart, the park benches where they sat — the benches

were the hardest, they were screwed down — all transported and rebuilt here on the estate! Thank heavens the two of them never visited the Eiffel Tower.
AMANDA. You must love your nephew very much.
DUCHESS. I adore him. *(Takes her hand.)* As will you. I decided since Albert prefers to have his hair cut at home and his nails trimmed at home, why not have his memories kept at home too?
AMANDA. But what has this got to do with me? I'm not a missing piece of your collection. I've never been to that café, I've never been to Dinard. I can provide documentation if need be.
DUCHESS. *(To Hector.)* Amusing, isn't she?
HECTOR. Sharp.
DUCHESS. Witty.
HECTOR. But sharp.
DUCHESS. Yes, yes, sharp. *(To Amanda.)* Ever since they lanced his boils, everybody is "sharp." *(To Hector.)* We must tell her why she's here. Tell her, Hector.
HECTOR. Me?
DUCHESS. Of course!
HECTOR. Why?
DUCHESS. You're a man.
HECTOR. No, I'm not.
DUCHESS. Why not?
HECTOR. Because you say I'm not.
DUCHESS. I take it back. You're a big, strong, leathery hairy man of a man. Now tell this child what we want.
HECTOR. I'll panic!
DUCHESS. And to think our family once defended a bridge against 2000 men with picks!
HECTOR. Some men *defend* a bridge, some men *play* bridge. I am the latter!
DUCHESS. I was wrong, Hector. You're not a big, hairy man, you're a little, squooshy man made of skin from a baby's bottom. Go be squooshy and hairless! I will rally the troops alone! *(Hector starts to leave. He stops and turns.)*
HECTOR. I have hair.
DUCHESS. GO AWAY! *(Hector goes off, muttering.)*
HECTOR. I've seen it in the mirror … *(The Duchess abandons*

her attitude of crushing contempt. She sits near Amanda and smiles.)
DUCHESS. We must seem strange. That's because we *are* strange. And what I'm about to ask you may make you want to run away again. Believe me, if you were my daughter that's what I'd tell you to do. I'd say, "Run away! Run away! That woman is crazy!" But I don't have a daughter. Gaston and I were never able to have children. Was it his fault, poor useless darling, or was it mine? Whatever the reason, I have no children. But I do have a nephew. And if I am extravagant, it's because I love him. Heaven gives us different burdens and so many roles, some small, some too silly to play. Mine ends with quite a twist, especially for someone of my background. But for you, sitting there with your whole life before you, it could be so easy to fulfill this one dream of a crazy old lady who is at the end of her tether.
AMANDA. I don't understand.
DUCHESS. You're not meant to. I chatter on so because I'm hoping the sun will set and you won't be able to see me blush when I ask you what I must! Oh, dear, I can feel my cheeks aflame already!
AMANDA. The sun has set, Madame.
DUCHESS. So it has. My child, have you had lovers?
AMANDA. Lovers?
DUCHESS. I'm not talking about "Love, the Eternal," "Love, the True." I'm talking about attraction without meaning. Kisses without thought. Embraces meant for a day, a night but not a lifetime. The frolic of the flesh that hasn't met the flutter of the heart.
AMANDA. *(Small voice.)* Of course, I've had lovers. But I have never ... loved.
DUCHESS. Well, life is full of unexpected treats. My Albert is a handsome boy, full of youth and charm that sleep behind his sadness ... And he is going to kill himself tomorrow.
AMANDA. Tomorrow!
DUCHESS. If he cannot get back his Léocadia. I bought him stones and plaster and fools who glimpsed her, but none of them, none of *us* know how to ease his torment or mend his heart. I am old, and despite the gains of democracy, insanely rich, yet I fear I will see Albert die without being able to lift a finger!
AMANDA. But, Madame, I don't understand what can I do for him!

DUCHESS. You don't see it? No one has ever told you?
AMANDA. Told me what?
DUCHESS. The moment I saw you in that hat shop I almost cried out! You are the very image of Léocadia! *(A silence.)*
AMANDA. I'm not her. And as for love and lovers … if I take a lover it is because my heart tells me to, not because it is a … a job! *(She grasps her little suitcase.)*
DUCHESS. Of course, my child. Forgive me. *(We hear the bell of a bicycle.)* It's him! Lean on that obelisk.
AMANDA. What — ?!
DUCHESS. It's where he saw her for the first time! Let him see you, if only this one time! Let him be awakened by the resemblance! Pretend it's the plot of a play! I beg you! He is handsome, charming, rich, witty and how many of your former and/or future lovers fit that description? All he needs is one moment of happiness. A happiness you hold in your hand! *(The bell rings again in the darkness, close.)*
AMANDA. What should I say?
DUCHESS. Say simply, "Excuse me, Monsieur, can you tell me the way to the sea?" *(The Duchess hides. The Prince, young, handsome and sad, enters on his bicycle. He passes very close to Amanda against the obelisk.)*
AMANDA. "Excuse me, Monsieur … " *(He stops, dismounts, takes off his hat.)*
PRINCE. Mademoiselle?
AMANDA. "Can you tell me the way to the sea?"
PRINCE. Second road on the left. *(He bows, gets on his bicycle and rides away. We hear the bell further off. The Duchess enters.)*
AMANDA. He didn't recognize me …
DUCHESS. Well … it was dark. The last train has gone. You'll stay the night?
AMANDA. Oui, Madame.

Scene 3

The solarium. The next morning. The cherub's fountain is streaming. The Headwaiter is seated, waiting. The Butler enters and snaps his finger at the fountain. The flow of water stops. The Headwaiter looks just like the Butler. They look at each other without warmth.

HEADWAITER. *(Icy.)* Good morning, Monsieur.
BUTLER. *(Icy as well.)* Monsieur, good morning. *(A moment while they inspect each other from head to toe. The Butler straightens the knot of his tie. In spite of himself, the Headwaiter makes the same gesture.)* And to what purpose may I surmise is your appearance here this morning, Monsieur?
HEADWAITER. The duchess summoned me, Monsieur, to discuss the fictive establishment I manage in the garden.
BUTLER. Well, then, in that case, Monsieur, I suppose I must offer you a seat.
HEADWAITER. *(Sits down stiffly.)* Thank you, Monsieur.
BUTLER. Not at all, Monsieur. A word, though, if I may. I have always been in service. Actually, if I may amend, I should say that in fact I have always been in service in the very best homes. But I have a brother-in-law, a perfectly decent man otherwise, who chose, because of what he referred to as "the money," to leave service for a career in the hotel business. He has been at the Piccardy, the Waldorf, the Savoy. You've heard of them, no doubt, Monsieur?
HEADWAITER. A bit, Monsieur.
BUTLER. Well, Monsieur, whenever I come into contact with colleagues of my brother-in-law, a contact mercifully infrequent, I have noticed a pronounced relaxation in their professional demeanor, a certain, shall we say, familiarity, which inevitably leads, even in those who have had the most exact training, to a tendency towards treating one's betters as clients instead of as masters.
HEADWAITER. Where is this going, Monsieur?

BUTLER. To *this*, Monsieur! Since circumstances have required me to make your acquaintance, I have NOT — and this to my great astonishment — noticed this defect in you, this familiarity-breeds-contempt malady of hotel management. I know you used to run an establishment in Dinard, albeit a short-lived one, which was not, as I understand, rated five stars, but —
HEADWAITER. *(Blurts, defensive.)* It was a good restaurant with a good clientele!
BUTLER. *(J'accuse!)* How many stars!
HEADWAITER. That's not — !
BUTLER. HOW MANY!
HEADWAITER. *(Meek, after a beat.)* ... Three.
BUTLER. *(Smug.)* I thought as much. Did it even have PLATES?! Monsieur, I do not want to believe that you are imitating me because I know that you know that any imitation could not possibly deceive an eye as practiced as mine. Yes. I'm that good. But so are you. No, Monsieur, I can only surmise that sometime in the not-so-distant past you yourself were in fact —
HEADWAITER. *(Cries to heaven.)* Yes! Yes! It's true! You've found me out! I was not always as you see me now! Once very long ago ... I too was ... a butler!
BUTLER. *(Holds up a hand.)* Enough, Monsieur. Far be it from me to pry loose the secret pain of your deep downfall. I am simply pleased to have it confirmed that in a true butler there always remains a foundation of manners that even a humiliating professional castration does not harm.
HEADWAITER. *(Teary and grateful.)* Thank you, Monsieur!
BUTLER. *(Noblesse oblige.)* It's nothing. Forgive me if I have rubbed coarse sea salt in your open, gaping wound. We will never speak of this again. Three stars! HA! *(The Butler leaves. The Duchess enters, followed by Hector and Amanda in a very Léocadia-like dress and accessories.)*
DUCHESS. There you are!
HEADWAITER. *(Rises.)* Madame, good morni —
DUCHESS. Don't say good morning! Look at this young woman; look at her well, look at her profoundly! What do you say now? *(The Headwaiter looks at Amanda, a little dumbfounded at first. Then suddenly he sees it.)*

HEADWAITER. Oop!
DUCHESS. "Oop!" *(Claps, jumps.)* Thank you, my friend, thank you for that "oop!" *(To Amanda.)* That "oop!" is a success! Now, you may say good morning.
HEADWAITER. Good morning, Madame.
DUCHESS. Good morning, my friend. *(Re: Amanda.)* Well, what do you think? A little disturbing, hm?
HEADWAITER. Scary.
DUCHESS. The very word for which I have searched in vain since yesterday evening. "Scary." Where did you find this word?
HEADWAITER. Er ... the dictionary?
DUCHESS. Ah, well, there it is. I never read. Still, it's the right word. "Scary." Boo! Don't fret, my dear, you may seem "scary" to us, but, in truth, you are a ... a what, Hector? Is she a Renoir? A Renoir that walks?
HECTOR. Fragonard.
DUCHESS. Pish-posh! She's not a bit rococo. A Fragonard brings to mind some frilly frock on a swing! A Renoir, though, or better yet a Degas, whose smile ... *when* she smiles ... amazes. Or a Daumier, a little waif lost in a Paris throng. *(To Amanda.)* Has anyone ever called you a Renoir-Degas-Daumier?
AMANDA. *(Naïve.)* No. Is that a kind of car?
DUCHESS. *(Beams.)* Precious!
HECTOR. Precious!
DUCHESS. *(Claps hands.)* All right, now! We have work to do. *(To Headwaiter.)* That is why I have summoned you to help us. When the prince sees this young lady, I want him to be rooted to the earth!
AMANDA. Oh, don't, Madame, I have terrible stage fright as it is!
DUCHESS. Now, now, we have a decided resemblance on our side. But resemblance is not enough, especially for a woman like Léocadia. We need an aura. *(Stops herself.)* The orchids! We forgot the orchids! Léocadia never went anywhere without a spray of orchids! It was her trademark. I must telephone Dinard and have a gross sent immediately. *(Duchess leaves; Hector follows her. Amanda remains alone with the Headwaiter. They look at each other for a moment.)*
AMANDA. So. You run the little café in the garden?

HEADWAITER. The Blue Danube? Oui, Mademoiselle.
AMANDA. Strange kind of work, isn't it?
HEADWAITER. There is no strange work, Mademoiselle, just strange workers.
AMANDA. Have you been doing this long? This ... "Café Memory?"
HEADWAITER. Two years.
AMANDA. Does it pay well?
HEADWAITER. *(Seemingly offended.)* Mademoiselle, the idea! This is a matter of great delicacy and discretion and ... *(Beat, giggles.)* Oui. *(Stiffens.)* Although that should not be taken as an affirmative.
AMANDA. Isn't it exhausting?
HEADWAITER. What, Mademoiselle?
AMANDA. Acting out a memory.
HEADWAITER. It's actually a fairly short workday.
AMANDA. What do you do the rest of the time?
HEADWAITER. Wait. Rearrange the place settings. Wait some more.
AMANDA. I only saw him for a moment yesterday. It was dark. Is he a nice prince?
HEADWAITER. Neither nice nor not nice. If pressed, I suppose I'd say he just doesn't seem to be "there."
AMANDA. What does he do when he comes to your café?
HEADWAITER. He sits at a table; always the same table — the table they sat at together — and he orders what they ordered, a Pommery Brut 1923. I serve it to him, with two glasses. Then he stares at the seat, sometimes for five minutes, sometimes the whole night long. Then he leaves and we drink his champagne.
AMANDA. Lucky you.
HEADWAITER. By the time I get it it's always flat.
AMANDA. *(Dreamy.)* They only knew each other three days. Doesn't it usually take longer?
HEADWAITER. What?
AMANDA. To fall in love.
HEADWAITER. *(Shrugs.)* It depends on the lighting.
AMANDA. Did they ... make love?
HEADWAITER. *(Recoils.)* If they did, it was not at my station!

Actually, the little hotel at Sainte-Anne-du-Pouldu claims that particular honor. But I think they made it up just to give them something to put on a plaque.
AMANDA. But even if they did it once ... well ... one is such a small number. Do you think he really is suffering?
HEADWAITER. Who can know what someone else suffers? One time, in Monte Carlo before the war, I witnessed the Grand Duke Zorotny reenact a tragic love affair by ordering three hundred bottles of Veuve Cliquot emptied into his suite and making two waiters dance a tarantella in it, while the Duke kept shouting to heaven: "Bertha von Clumberhoffen! If only I'd known you couldn't swim!"
(The Duchess, followed by Hector, enters.)
DUCHESS. Voilà! I will have two hundred orchids in ten minutes!
AMANDA. That's a lot of orchids.
DUCHESS. It's a lot, but not necessarily enough. Léocadia chewed orchids all day long. Do you know how long it takes for a person to chew through three dozen fully grown orchids?
AMANDA. No.
HECTOR. Less time than you'd think.
DUCHESS. *(Claps hands.)* Let's rehearse while we wait for the flowers. We shall attempt to reconstruct for this child the arrival of Léocadia at the Blue Danube. First our décor. Sit there. *(Pulls out chair.)*
AMANDA. Shall I try to take on a distinguished air?
DUCHESS. No, we'll handle the airs. You know, the more I think about it, the more I think the special allure of Léocadia was in her eyes. She had a way of looking at you that had an incomparable charm. Between the two of us, she was nearsighted. Practice blinking; it will be your first lesson. *(Looks at fountain.)* Léocadia claimed our marble-endowed cherub was the light and mocking spirit of the morning. I don't like the way it's looking at me. See to it, my friend.
HEADWAITER. Oui, Madame. *(The Headwaiter goes to the pissoir and blindfolds it.)*
DUCHESS. Much better. *(To Amanda.)* Blink, blink, tilt your head. Ooo. That last one was almost good. *(The Butler enters with a file. Amanda tilts her head and blinks.)*
BUTLER. Madame, you wanted these?

DUCHESS. Ah! *(To Amanda.)* My dear, these will prove invaluable.
AMANDA. What are they?
BUTLER. "The script."
DUCHESS. The Bible. The map. The blueprint for all we do here.
BUTLER. *(Going through the file.)* Things the prince said to the lady. Witticisms. Time line. Menus and recipes. Clothing sketches. Hand props. An artist's renditions of famous scenes from their three day courtship.
AMANDA. Heavens!
BUTLER. Guard it with what passes for your life. *(The Butler hands Amanda the file. He exits.)*
DUCHESS. Call this the stage for the musicians. And this the table where they sat. Is that about right?
HEADWAITER. Approximately, Madame.
DUCHESS. *(To Amanda.)* You may stop blinking, now, you'll develop a twitch. *(To Headwaiter.)* Now, my friend, it would be invaluable if you could expound for a bit on the impression the "Divine Léocadia" made on you when first she entered the Blue Danube. Amanda, stop blinking, you'll go blind.
AMANDA. *(Still blinking.)* I can't help myself.
DUCHESS. Lack of control. Good. You're starting to *become* her! *(To Headwaiter.)* We're waiting.
HEADWAITER. Well, to be frank, Madame, when Mademoiselle Léocadia Gardi entered my café the first time, I must confess … I just went all floofy!
DUCHESS. "Floofy." Interesting.
HEADWAITER. You see, Mademoiselle Léocadia had a way of walking, a way of looking you in the eye as if she didn't quite see you … perhaps it was shyness, perhaps it was arrogance.
DUCHESS. It's true. Léocadia would get so close you'd swear she was going to acknowledge your presence. Of course then, that unfocused gaze business would veer her off again, but … she also had a grace of movement. I don't have grace. I'm short and tend to bounce a lot like a bunny. But I like myself and that's what counts! *(To Headwaiter.)* Now comes the hard part!
HEADWAITER. Madame?
DUCHESS. *Do* Léocadia.
HEADWAITER. Pardon, Madame?

DUCHESS. Do Léocadia entering the Blue Danube.
HEADWAITER. *(Vamps.)* Oh. I don't know, Madame. Not in front of other people ...
DUCHESS. *(To Amanda.)* You have to beg him. *(To Headwaiter.)* Won't you please?
HEADWAITER. *(Bats his eyes.)* I couldn't.
DUCHESS. Please?
HEADWAITER. No, no.
DUCHESS. All right, forget it —
HEADWAITER. *(Eager after all.)* Well, if you insist! When Mademoiselle Léocadia Gardi entered the café, the orchestra had just begun to play a song, one that was quite popular among the young people that season. It was called: "Where Went the Waltz that Went With Love."
DUCHESS. Hector, you know "Where Went the Waltz that Went With Love." You sang it day and night that summer.
HECTOR. Well, you know how it is when you get a tune in your head.
DUCHESS. Well, we need to set the mood. Sing it.
HECTOR. Sing it? Oh, goody! *(To Amanda.)* I'm a very good singer!
HEADWAITER. If Madame permits, I shall commence.
DUCHESS. By all means.
HEADWAITER. Orchestra!
HECTOR. That's me! *(Hector attacks "Where Went the Waltz That Went with Love." The Headwaiter begins to mime solemnly the haughty entrance of Léocadia into the Blue Danube. At this moment, the Butler opens the door suddenly as if he has something urgent to say.)*
BUTLER. Madame — ! *(He stops, rooted in place. The Headwaiter is doing his impersonation of Léocadia and it's quite a show.)*
DUCHESS. That's it! The man's a mime! Keep going! *(The Headwaiter does a little flip movement with his leg and eyes, a dance-like gesture that has a certain camp violence to it, like a crazy dance step.)* BRAVO! Do that little flip movement again. Watch this! I love this part! Keep going! Go, my dear, follow him! *(The Headwaiter does the flip movement again, throwing himself into the role with incredible flair, as he parades about. Amanda walks behind him, imitating him and the flip. The Headwaiter finishes and turns to her,*

coaching her:)
HEADWAITER. Brava, Mademoiselle! Don't move too much. Mademoiselle Léocadia was not one for wiggling. And now right towards me, staring into my eyes and suddenly ... insolence! The eyes say it all: "You are but a headwaiter! You are nothing! You are dirt! Begone, I tell you! Begone! BE — !" *(The Prince enters and pushes aside the Butler who had stayed transfixed since his entrance without speaking a word. The Prince is pale with rage. Hector stops, the Duchess and the Headwaiter turn around, frightened. The Prince glares at Amanda, the last to see him standing there.)*
PRINCE. *WHAT IS THIS FARCE?!*
DUCHESS. Albert! Theophilus, I gave specific instructions that —
BUTLER. I came to warn you, Madame. But when I saw what was going on, I suffered a temporary but paralyzing stroke!
DUCHESS. *(To Butler and Headwaiter.)* Both of you! Go away! *(The Butler and the Headwaiter dash off.)*
PRINCE. Aunt? What do you think you're doing?
DUCHESS. *(Cowed.)* Well, to be truthful —
PRINCE. Leave, please.
DUCHESS. You want us all to go?
PRINCE. No. Just you and Uncle Hector. I want to talk to this young woman alone. *(Hector makes a rapid retreat. The Duchess prepares to leave.)* Who did this to the fountain?
DUCHESS. It was me, Albert, I —
PRINCE. Didn't I leave instructions that no one must, under any pretext, touch what she had touched! *(The Duchess leaves while making complicitous gestures to Amanda behind the Prince's back. To Amanda.)* I fear my aunt has put you in an awkward situation, Mademoiselle.
AMANDA. *(No fear.)* I fear too, Monsieur.
PRINCE. You must have needed work badly to agree to this charade.
AMANDA. Your aunt took great care, even before summoning me here, to use her influence to have me dismissed from the house of fashion that had previously employed me.
PRINCE. Amazing woman, my aunt.
AMANDA. Hmm. Although since arriving here yesterday, very little amazes me anymore.
PRINCE. You arrived yesterday?

AMANDA. *(Nods.)* We met last night actually. In the garden, near the obelisk.
PRINCE. *(Blinks.)* That was *you?* I beg your pardon. It was dark. Why did you ask me the way to the sea?
AMANDA. I was asked to ask you.
PRINCE. *(Closes his eyes.)* "Excuse me, Monsieur … Can you tell me the way to the sea?" *(He goes to sit in an armchair; he no longer says anything, he dreams. The silence continues. Amanda coughs, makes some noise; nothing works. She starts to exit on tiptoes.)* Don't leave! Come here, stand there, in front of me! Appearance, rather plebeian. Accent, Paris, lower class, Montparnasse, I should think. How could I have been fooled? You don't look like her. You could never look like her. No one can look like her. You're a … shopgirl. You have no mystery, no aura.
AMANDA. What exactly is "aura?"
PRINCE. Mademoiselle, if you want lessons in vocabulary, you have come to the wrong prince.
AMANDA. I only want to know if it's an insult.
PRINCE. *(After a beat; softens.)* No, it's not an insult.
AMANDA. Good.
PRINCE. What would you have done if it had been an insult?
AMANDA. I would have said what I think of you.
PRINCE. *(Turns away, weary.)* I don't care what anyone thinks of me. *(He curls himself up into his armchair. Amanda watches him with pity in her eyes. The Prince's eyes close.)* "Can you tell me the way … " *(Stops; pause; softer.)* "Can you tell me the way … " *(Stops; searching for another tone.)* "Can you tell me the way to the … " *(Stops. Amanda, who has tears in her eyes, murmurs behind him like in the preceding scene.)*
AMANDA. "Can you tell me the way to the sea?" *(The Prince's eyes open.)*
PRINCE. *(Gentle.)* Who taught you to imitate her voice in that way?
AMANDA. No one. It's my own voice.
PRINCE. *(After a beat; closes eyes.)* Say that sentence again, once more, please.
AMANDA. "Can you tell me the way to the sea?"
PRINCE. *(Eyes closed.)* "Second road on your left, Mademoiselle."

AMANDA. Thank you, Monsieur. *(Amanda starts off.)*
PRINCE. *(Eyes still closed.)* "Mademoiselle!" *(Amanda stops.)* "You dropped your glove." *(Amanda looks at her feet, surprised, then she understands that he is thinking of his meeting two years ago.)*
AMANDA. *(Slightly flustered.)* Thank you, Monsieur. Thank you very much.
PRINCE. *(Opens eyes — crisp.)* WRONG! She didn't answer me! She only smiled a little smile and then she was gone. Into the dark, into the night. *(He stands up and wipes something on his cheek.)* I beg your pardon.
AMANDA. It's me who begs your pardon, Monsieur, for being here. What I don't understand is that last night you answered me so calmly, as if people asked you the way to the sea all the time.
PRINCE. Strange, isn't it? *(Looks away.)* Mademoiselle. I know I haven't been at my best this morning. And despite the fact that you'll agree when I say my aunt has what one might call an "eccentric" bent ... would you consider accepting her proposal? For a while at least? For, say, three days.
AMANDA. *(Angry and confused.)* Last night I said no. This morning I said all right. A moment ago it was no again.
PRINCE. Go for four. It'll make it even.
AMANDA. Do I look like a fool?
PRINCE. Do I?
AMANDA. ... Foolishness becomes you. I can't afford it.
PRINCE. What's the worst that could happen if you "played" a fool?
AMANDA. The worst? My stockings would run, I'd lose my gloves, I'd lose my job and miss my trains. Of course since that's already happened, I'm ahead of the game.
PRINCE. You know what my aunt has created here. For someone like you, it must be irritating to see so much money, time and effort wasted on the worship of a memory.
AMANDA. No. When the soldier came to our house and gave us the telegram that said Papa wouldn't be coming back from the war, my mother took to sleeping in the kitchen, on a cot. She had made the bedroom into a shrine to my father, everything he owned, she laid out. The suit he wore on their wedding day lay next to her white dress on their bed; and every year, on the anniversary of his

death, she spent more of her income on chrysanthemums than you could ever spend to rebuild a whole town. Comparatively.
PRINCE. I apologize.
AMANDA. You needn't.
PRINCE. Actually I'm quite pleased by what you've just confided, for it allows me to make my own confession, one I've never made to anyone. My aunt is mad, charmingly mad, but mad all the same. I, on the other hand, am sane. I even have what is commonly known as common sense. But if I have put up with her madness, her folly, her furious building and painting and decorating … it is because I have hoped that all this artifice might help. I clutch at this memory because I fear I've already begun to forget.
AMANDA. Forget…?
PRINCE. The woman I love. You see, I'm not even sure anymore of the color of her eyes. Or the tenor of her voice. *(Cuts off, looks away.)* The world is right to mock me. Prince Albert Troubiscoi has constructed a whole town in his garden to remember his love, only he no longer recalls the first sentence she said to him. *(He collapses into his seat, despondent.)*
AMANDA. What can I do for you, Monsieur?
PRINCE. *(Looks away, in pain.)* Stay here three days. Let me look at you as I looked at her. It will be in vain, I assure you. But *try,* I beg you, *try* to be someone else. Try to fool me. Try to be her … for three days.
AMANDA. I shall, Monsieur. *(The Prince turns and sees her. He jumps up and cries out.)*
PRINCE. Don't move! The day after we met she came to the chateau to ask my aunt if she would let her use our garden for a charity ball. My aunt had gone out, so I received her. There she was, just as you are now. She told me that she rather fancied my fountain. We passed the whole afternoon together, and that evening she allowed me to accompany her to the Blue Danube, where the next day we discovered we were in love. *(Closes his eyes again.)* The Blue Danube. The most ridiculous café in the world. With that ridiculous waiter and those gypsies playing that ridiculous music she kept singing all night long … *(He croons the beginning of the waltz awkwardly:)*

That night we vowed we'd never part,

But fate was deaf to my sweetheart.
We waltzed and waltzed …
AMANDA.
But then you somehow waltzed away.
PRINCE and AMANDA.
Where I wonder went the waltz
With my love?"
(As Amanda and the Prince gaze at each other, the orchestra takes over. The lights dim.)

ACT TWO

Scene 1

The Blue Danube, a gypsy café, illuminated with rococo chandeliers and rustic charm. A stage upstage center. Four gypsies loll about the café. They are: Maria, Nikos, Flagel and Peshke. Maria is sitting downstage with Nikos, playing cards. Flagel tries to balance his violin bow on his nose. Peshke sprawls on a table, playing the clarinet. A noise off. Flagel signals the others downstage. They leap up to the stage, striking up a wild gypsy melody. The Headwaiter enters, smoking a cigarette. The gypsies stop playing, with a "oh, it's just you" reaction. Nikos gripes to the Headwaiter.

NIKOS. Say, don't you know you should never cross a gypsy?!
HEADWAITER. *(Mutters.)* Yeah, you're a gypsy like I'm a longshoreman ... *(Maria and Nikos go back downstage to play cards, Flagel goes back to his nose act, and Peshke goes back to diddling on the clarinet. Headwaiter opens his newspaper and starts to read, puffing on his cigarette. Suddenly another gypsy, Bela, dashes in and signals offstage.)*
BELA. PSSST! They're here!
OTHERS. What?
BELA. They're here! Romeo and the dead girl lookalike! *(The gypsies scramble to the stage again and start playing. The Headwaiter stashes the paper and puts out his cigarette in a flowerpot, waving the smoke away. Then he takes up his "perfect maitre d'" position. Amanda and the Prince enter in evening dress. Amanda wears gobs of jewels. She enters like she's been taught to: à la Léocadia, including the famous, haughty "flip movement." They sit at "their table." The Headwaiter rushes to them.)*
HEADWAITER. Ah, good evening, Monsieur, Mademoiselle.

What shall I bring, eh?
PRINCE. The same as last night.
HEADWAITER. Very good, Monsieur. *(Jots note.)* A Pommery Brut 1923.
AMANDA. And could I get a Pernod with some water? *(The music stops. Everyone but Amanda looks stunned.)*
HEADWAITER. ... Er ...
AMANDA. *(Suddenly embarrassed, giggles.)* Oh! I'm sorry, I forgot! *(Soberly.)* Ahem. "Champagne, please, same as yesterday." *(The music starts again, relieved.)*
PRINCE. *(A little stiffly, after a moment.)* You know, if you really want Pernod, he'll bring it to you.
HEADWAITER. *(Panic-stricken.)* Well, actually, Monsieur, I don't know that we have any. *(Whispers.)* It's not in the script. *(Louder.)* Nevertheless, I shall see if I can find some. If Mademoiselle desires a Pernod, I shall seek out a Pernod.
AMANDA. And some water! Please?
HEADWAITER. Water? Water has never come up before!
AMANDA. Oh, you must have water.
HEADWAITER. No! No, we don't! We've never needed it.
AMANDA. How could you not have...?
HEADWAITER. *(Sucks it in.)* No, no. One serves one's betters as one would serve a master, not a client. If Mademoiselle desires a Pernod with water, I shall procure a Pernod with water. Somehow. *(Headwaiter exits.)*
AMANDA. *(Excusing herself with a smile.)* It's hard not to want what you want. I mean, for two whole days to have to follow a —
PRINCE. *(A little curtly.)* It's almost over. By tomorrow night, you'll be gone.
AMANDA. It's tricky to play ... to be another woman. *(Re: jewels, etc.)* Especially a woman so rich, so loved. *(The Headwaiter has been whispering with the musicians. It's all very anxious and animated. Then Bela snaps his fingers.)*
BELA. I have Pernod! *(Bela opens his violin case and takes out a nearly empty bottle of Pernod. The Headwaiter takes it and cues the musicians to play. The musicians start to play a frenetic gypsy tune. While the gypsies play, the Headwaiter gets a bucket of ice and — in a frenzy of comic improvisation — melts the ice in his hands, under*

his armpits, between his knees, etc. As the tune comes to an end, he has somehow made the Pernod with water and — on the last notes — plops the glass in front of Amanda.)
HEADWAITER. Why, look what I found! A Pernod. With some water. Don't spill it.
AMANDA. *(Who is really thirsty.)* Ah! Thank you. I was going to die of thirst! *(She swallows the drink in one gulp, grimaces because it's too strong and almost chokes. She gives her glass to the Headwaiter.)*
HEADWAITER. Voilà.
PRINCE. Voilà.
AMANDA. Voilà.
PRINCE. Now that all that is over, about yesterday … *(And the orchestra, which had for a moment suspended its breath, strikes up the "waltz." A singing gypsy steps forward.)*
SINGING GYPSY.
    Where went the waltz that went with love?
    Where went the charms of stars above?
    Where went the flame that danced in her eyes?
    Where went the love that left only sighs?
    Where went the scent of sweet perfume?
    Where went the light that lit the room?
    Where went the kiss that tasted of wine?
    Where went the lips that parted from mine?
    We met that evening in the park.
    Your gaze met mine, and then we knew.
    We floated down the river.
    Sun gave way to dark.
    Gold gave way to red
    And finally to blue.
    That night we vowed we'd never part,
    But fate was deaf to my sweetheart.
    We waltzed and waltzed,
    But then you somehow waltzed away.
    Where I wonder went the waltz
    With my love?
(As they play, the Headwaiter, who had prepared his champagne bucket, brings it, and, with other ceremonious gestures, succeeds in serving it.)
PRINCE. Now. Where were we?

AMANDA. Er ... You were speaking about yesterday.
PRINCE. Oh, yes. I was hoping you'd gotten over yesterday. Any mistakes, I mean. You weren't altogether bad, you know. First time, of course, and certainly not without your share of snags, blunders, et cetera, but for all the errors, the lapses in manners, the quality of being somehow completely conventional in a normal sort of way, you were, well, rather adequate.
AMANDA. *(Not sure this is a compliment.)* Thank you.
PRINCE. Not at all. On you, adequacy is more than adequate. Of course, one must make allowances for the difference in upbringing, education, class —
AMANDA. *(Counters.)* I didn't speak any slang!
PRINCE. Ah, but that's just it. Léocadia spoke only in slang. And very much her own particular brand of slang. One needed a translator just to go around with her. Couldn't reconstruct it if I had a phrase book. May I tell you the part I liked best about last night?
AMANDA. Please.
PRINCE. The part where you ate the flowers.
AMANDA. *(Excuses herself, embarrassed.)* Ah. You know, I don't usually throw up like that.
PRINCE. We probably should've mentioned she never swallowed them, just chewed.
AMANDA. I suppose I'm not really used to such things. Which is why I ... "became indisposed." Today has been better, hasn't it?
PRINCE. Leaps and bounds! That bit on the boat this afternoon, while we were rowing up the river, doing nothing ... well, there were times that you almost seemed to become her.
AMANDA. *(Happy.)* Really?
PRINCE. When you were silent, when your head was bobbing, when the sun was in your eyes and your expression was stunned and dulled and rather vacant-looking, you had her completely.
AMANDA. *(Not sure that's a compliment either.)* Thank you.
PRINCE. Of course, Léocadia wasn't stupid, she was quite, quite brilliant, in her way. But she made a decided effort to disguise it.
AMANDA. Uh-huh.
PRINCE. I don't think I ever once witnessed her recognize a book title, use a word over two syllables, or react to loud noises. It was her strategy to put you at ease. She was very good at it.

AMANDA. But if she was so good at playing dumb how did you know it was an act?
PRINCE. It was the only explanation! At any rate, if I may say again, this afternoon you were perfect. A little too lively, perhaps, a little too active, but —
AMANDA. I'll be better at the inactivity part this evening. Especially if we have another "light" meal like we've been having. The less I eat, the weaker I become, and the weaker I become, the more inactive I'll be.
PRINCE. Léocadia never consumed food. When we dined, she would place her glove on her plate.
AMANDA. Yes, I know. I almost ate mine last night.
PRINCE. *(Suspicious.)* You're not having food sent up to your room, are you?
AMANDA. Monsieur! I wouldn't dream of doing that ... even though among the many differences between Mademoiselle Gardi and me is that whereas she no longer has need of food, I do. When you and I are together all I have is champagne, orchids and gloves. I used to go to bed before sunset, now I stay up till dawn, not eating and not thinking about eating.
PRINCE. Aren't you off duty by then?
AMANDA. Oui, but I try to stay in character. It'll be different after tomorrow. I'll sleep then.
PRINCE. Why after tomorrow?
AMANDA. *(Becomes flustered.)* Because tomorrow we ... Well, until a job is done, I like to do it properly, that's all. *(They turn away from each other, embarrassed. The gypsies immediately take up their instruments and play another tune. When the Prince starts talking again they finish softly and sit down.)*
PRINCE. Well. It is still the second evening and not the last, so I suggest we get back to that, hm?
AMANDA. It was the second evening that you both knew you were in love?
PRINCE. *(Brusquely.)* Who told you that?
AMANDA. I don't know. You?
PRINCE. It was not me, it would never have been me!
AMANDA. Perhaps I just assumed.
PRINCE. Why?

AMANDA. ... It just feels that if two people were to fall in love, now would be when it would happen.
PRINCE. Hm. Well. As it happens, you're right, it *was* the second evening. And as the second night unfurled with its music, its wine, its talk ...
AMANDA. What did you talk about that night?
PRINCE. Us. Her houses. Her hats. Her scarves. But the talk was always about us.
AMANDA. Who spoke? You or her?
PRINCE. Both of us. But if one were forced to quantify it, I suppose she spoke rather a bit more. Why do you ask?
AMANDA. No reason. It's just ... if I'd fallen in love with you at the end of a long, hot afternoon of water and sunlight, I would've wanted to cool myself inside a satin gown, with only the chill of these diamonds on my arms and a cold glass in my hand, and gaze at you, without saying a word.
PRINCE. Well, that's because you're not as self-analytical as she. Léocadia had so much to be analyzed. She saw three separate analysts six times a week.
AMANDA. That's eighteen times a week.
PRINCE. She was trying to discover if she had a subconscious.
AMANDA. I've never had an analyst. I have a cat.
PRINCE. You're not by nature talkative?
AMANDA. Oh, I love to talk! At the first shop I worked in, the other girls called me "The Mouth."
PRINCE. The Mouth?
AMANDA. Because mine was always open.
PRINCE. Ah.
AMANDA. *(Laughs.)* In the shop after that they called me "The Foot."
PRINCE. Foot?
AMANDA. *(Giggles.)* Because mine was always in my mouth.
PRINCE. *(After a beat.)* ... Foot/Mouth. Clever. You don't seem to have your foot in your mouth this evening.
AMANDA. *(Giggles again.)* If I get any hungrier I will!
PRINCE. Pardon?
AMANDA. *(Smiles, calms down.)* Monsieur, if I'm not putting my foot in my mouth it's because I want this evening to be nice for

you. If I can speak like Mademoiselle Gardi, but maybe I can *not* speak like her, too.
PRINCE. What do you mean?
AMANDA. There are so many ways for a woman to be silent while listening to a man talk, especially the man she loves. What was hers?
PRINCE. She spoke less loudly.
AMANDA. *(Blinks.)* Her way of being silent was to speak less loudly?
PRINCE. In relative terms. She was too full of words not to speak. You'd ask her a question, she'd answer it, hours later she'd still be speaking, but the subject had changed a thousand times, one path leading to another path leading to a road leading to another road until you'd suddenly find yourself asking "Where are we?"
AMANDA. Did she ever ask you a question?
PRINCE. She'd ask a question … and then she'd answer it. And then hours later …
AMANDA. "Where are we?"
PRINCE. Which is not to say you couldn't attempt a response, but you had to get in there fast. And even then she'd usually —
AMANDA. — finish your sentence?
PRINCE. Sometimes, there wasn't even the give and take of actual conversation. Sometimes she'd just murmur disjointed words, usually Rumanian ones, which was her native tongue, and that was a tad difficult since I don't understand Rumanian, but she never seemed to mind if you didn't understand. Her conversation was like a fountain. And her laugh! It was a very throaty laugh. And very abrupt! She'd suddenly burst out laughing in the middle of a conversation, at the most inappropriate times. I'd say, "My mother died that summer." Laugh, laugh, laugh!
AMANDA. I must seem very calm to you.
PRINCE. You could never mimic the way she spoke! No one could've written any of it down for you to study. Most of it was unintelligible. But when you're still, when you're silent, when your face … *(He takes her hand very naturally. Then he realizes what he's done. He drops it.)* Oh! Excuse me!
AMANDA. *(Dumbfounded, looks at her hand.)* Why?
PRINCE. I forgot!

AMANDA. What?
PRINCE. I touched your hand.
AMANDA. So?
PRINCE. She hated to be touched.
AMANDA. By?
PRINCE. Anyone.
AMANDA. Including you?
PRINCE. Especially me! She said I had the grasp of a monkey! Rough hands disturbed her.
AMANDA. *(Brusquely takes his hand; looks at it.)* Rough…?
PRINCE. *(A little embarrassed, his hand prisoner.)* I have calluses. Yachting, tennis, polo. What are you doing?
AMANDA. *(Who looks at his hand.)* Comparing the difference between a worker's calluses and the calluses of a man of leisure.
PRINCE. So what is the difference?
AMANDA. *(Wry.)* Choice.
PRINCE. You have calluses?
AMANDA. Hm-hm. See? *(He takes her hand. She closes her eyes.)* Your hands are strong, but they're not rough. *(The Prince pulls back his hand. There is a silence. The gypsies pick up their instruments again. The first violin comes down to their table to play his most amorous tune. The Prince looks at his hand. At the end of a moment, Amanda ventures timidly.)* What are you thinking?
PRINCE. I'm thinking that if Léocadia had said to me about my hand what you did just now, I would have been mad with happiness.
AMANDA. But she talked so much, she must have told you … she must have told you that she loved you.
PRINCE. *(Hedges.)* Well … amid her downpour of conversation, it's hard to recall the exact words.
AMANDA. "I love you."
PRINCE. Well, true, those are exact words. But she was so alight that evening! She talked about everything, anything, nothing! She'd cut herself off in the middle of a heartfelt moment, then play a scene from some forgotten opera! She'd be Helen, I'd be Menelaus, she'd be Clytemnestra, I'd be Agamemnon. By the time we got to coffee, I'd been every spurned lover in history. She even made me light up this enormous cigar under the pretext that I be Zeus disguised as a cloud of blue smoke! I think I was also

Siegfried and some moloch from Wagner, but maybe the smoke just made me dizzy. *(The music gently stops. In the silence, Amanda asks in a small, plain voice.)*
AMANDA. But she never said … "I love you"?
PRINCE. *(Ill-humored.)* Léocadia never would have said something as banal and uninteresting as "I love you"! She never said "I love you" in her whole life, not to anyone, not to anything, not even to her pet dog or that stupid little snake which followed her everywhere!
AMANDA. She never once said, "I love you, Albert"?
PRINCE. *(Whose ill humor is growing.)* "I love you, Albert"! What is that? "I love you, Albert, I love you, Albert, I love you, Albert"! Say it too often, it loses all meaning!
AMANDA. But she didn't say it *once.*
PRINCE. Understand this, once and for all: What happened here was not the stuff of sentimental women's fiction! It's not a magazine story about some hat-maker and a shoe clerk who meet waiting for the metro to come!
AMANDA. Maybe she said "I love you," and you missed it.
PRINCE. I didn't miss a thing! *(Quieter.)* I listened very carefully.
AMANDA. Maybe she said it in Rumanian.
PRINCE. That was the one Rumanian phrase I took the trouble to learn.
AMANDA. Before I came … when you would come here in the evening and sit and be served champagne and listen to music … would you try to conjure her image sitting across from you?
PRINCE. Oui.
AMANDA. And when you did … could you hear her speak? In your imagination?
PRINCE. Sometimes. It takes several hours before I can even conjure her face. It's hard to keep her still long enough just to get the features right. Sometimes all I can manage is a blur. But then sometimes she seems to slow down for a moment and rest. And when she does, and I feel I have her in my sights, I try to make her speak. I make her say very simple things. "Oui." "No." "Don't touch me." I make her say my name too. She gave me the strangest names: Paris the Shepherd; Jo-jo, the Mute; Eine Kleiner Swan-Boy. She never called me by my actual name. She said it was stupid. So, I

have my revenge. I make her say "Albert" all night long, I make her repeat: "Albert, don't pout." "Albert, don't touch me." "Albert, my dear Albert." That last is rather a cheat, because the only time she ever said "dear" was to mock me.
AMANDA. But you never make her say: "I love you."
PRINCE. *(Bows his head, uncomfortable.)* I can't imagine her saying it. I can't even make her mouth form the words.
AMANDA. *(Tenderly.)* Look at me. *(He raises his head, surprised, looks at her.)* I love you, Albert. I love you, Albert. Look at my mouth. Remember it. I love you, Albert.
PRINCE. *(His throat knotted.)* Thank you. *(He wants to pour the champagne, but his hand is trembling. He fails. The Headwaiter, who is watching him, comes quickly, mistaking the incompleted gesture.)*
HEADWAITER. More champagne, Monsieur?
PRINCE. Please. *(The Headwaiter removes the bucket. At that moment the orchestra, which seems to have been waiting for this signal, attacks a lively piece. The Prince gets up, suddenly furious.)* Stop! Stop playing that music! *(The musicians stop, dumbfounded.)*
HEADWAITER. Pardon, Monsieur. But Monsieur cannot have forgotten that when more champagne is ordered, the musicians play that song. It's on page forty-seven.
PRINCE. *(Exasperated.)* I don't want the music! How often must I tell you!
HEADWAITER. Not often! Less than once! Never! *(The gypsies tremble. The Headwaiter trembles, shaking the bottle he holds. The Prince and Amanda look at each other, hostile. The Headwaiter, who trembles more and more, lets the cork pop.)* My apologies, Monsieur! I'll get another one!
AMANDA. And another Pernod with water.
HEADWAITER. Another Pernod with ... oui. *(Goes off.)*
PRINCE. Why are you acting like this?
AMANDA. I'm not acting anything. You're the one in a foul mood, and there's no reason for a foul mood, at least according to the script. So, until you get back to the outline, I'm going to go back to being "me" for a moment. In addition to which, *I'm* thirsty. In addition to which, *I* don't like champagne.
PRINCE. "I"! "I"! Everything with you is "I"! For two whole days you have not ceased being "you"! Go ahead, laugh at me, like every-

one else, laugh at something you couldn't possibly understand!
AMANDA. *(Snaps at him.)* Excuse me! I'm on break! *(Amanda goes to the bar. Pause as the Prince shifts uncomfortably.)*
PRINCE. You thought it was funny to say ... those words, didn't you?
AMANDA. What words?
PRINCE. The words she never said to me!
AMANDA. *(Shouts.)* "I love you!"
PRINCE. Stop! You know they hurt me, and still you insist on saying them!
AMANDA. I thought it might do you some good.
PRINCE. You're lying.
AMANDA. All right, I'm lying. And I apologize for what I'm about to say because it's going to hurt. Suffering from love is so precious that one doesn't have the right to waste it on something like this. Voilà! Now what are you going to do? Fire me? If I go back to Paris, I go back to Paris, but at least I will have told you the truth: *She didn't love you!* Deep in your heart, you've known that from the first. And there's something else: You are young, rich, handsome, charming and your hands are not rough. You should live. You should be happy. Forget the script! Because the truth that you won't admit to me or to yourself is — *you — didn't — love — her — either. (There is a silence. Everyone has suspended his/her breath. Then the Prince says in a calm voice:)*
PRINCE. Waiter.
HEADWAITER. Monsieur!
PRINCE. Mademoiselle's wrap, please.
HEADWAITER. Oui, Monsieur!
PRINCE. The path back to the chateau is that way. Present your bill for payment to my aunt tomorrow morning.
AMANDA. You mention money to hurt me, but it doesn't hurt me, it hurts you.
PRINCE. Oh, your performance was done out of charity? I had forgotten how noble is the common citizen! If you insist on your shopgirl's noblesse oblige, we'll be happy to oblige.
AMANDA. The only payment I want is the price of a return ticket and three days' milliner wages at union scale. I can let you know what that is if you happen not to. *(The Headwaiter comes forward with*

Amanda's cloak.)
HEADWAITER. Mademoiselle's wrap.
AMANDA. That's not mine. *I* don't wear furs in the summer! In the summer, *I'm* HOT! *(Amanda is about to leave with dignity.)*
PRINCE. *(His voice stops her.)* Mademoiselle! I know I am of a class from which the grand comic tradition of farce recruits its stock characters, its frauds and fools. I was raised in a world of old ladies and retainers and never had much, if any, contact with what you might call ... life. I was born to limitations, and if that warrants calling me a fool, fine!
AMANDA. I never said you were a fool.
PRINCE. You wanted to very loudly! Go ahead! Call me a fool! But know this: A fool is just a name for someone you don't understand. Your type sit in cafés and complain about the oppression of the masses, but I'll wager it's never occurred to you that a prince can be oppressed!
AMANDA. You're right, that had not occurred to me.
PRINCE. Do you know what it's like to grow up in a monument to the sixteenth century? Do you know what it's like to have twenty-two names accompanied by a series of titles that lost all significance before the invention of the belt buckle? Every time I went into Dinard the children mocked me behind my back, for the way I walked and bowed and tipped my hat. Find a village idiot and discover he can spell, they give him a scholarship and make him President of the Republic, but grow up an aristocrat and you have to be a genius just to stay on par!
AMANDA. What do you want to say to me?
PRINCE. I am not a fool!
AMANDA. Fine.
PRINCE. And neither are you!
AMANDA. Better.
PRINCE. But you can't believe I could have loved a person as "foolish" as Léocadia Gardi.
AMANDA. ... I never said she was "foolish."
PRINCE. Well, of course you didn't say it, you're a sensitive little shopgirl, you believe the dead are sacred! But if she were here tonight you'd laugh at her out loud, wouldn't you?
AMANDA. Not out loud.

PRINCE. But therein lies the paradox. If I am not a fool, how then could I have loved her? Sit down.
AMANDA. Why?
PRINCE. Because I'm going to embark on a soliloquy. *(Amanda sits.)* Many a memory is beautiful, but most of life is not. The catch is: To get to the memory you have to live the life first. And my life, from the first recollection I have, was always a fog. Dull, gray, oppressive, thick. The sky was never blue. The sun was never bright. The waters never sparkled, and the fountains only dripped. I'm not making a special case for myself; I assumed all life was like this, for everyone. One simply must find a way of dealing with it. So I made a list. You can sleep through life. But then you wake. You can drink through it. But then you sober up. You can smoke opium and take cocaine. But the effect is brief. I asked various exemplars for advice: A Boy Scout leader prescribed, "Good cheer, fortitude, exercise and very cold showers at dawn." A priest counseled, "Humility, acceptance and three confessions six times a week." A businessman said, "Lose yourself in ambition." But I didn't have one. An artist said, "Lose yourself in yourself." But I wasn't convinced there was a self in which I could disappear. A playboy said, "Pursue pleasure." But pleasure I found is a full-time job. One man, a philanthropist, said that I should throw myself into altruistic pursuits: volunteer work, committees for the beautification of things that weren't beautiful. That distracted me for a while. But there was always a moment when the distractions died down, and there I was again … in the fog. The only thing left for me seemed to be nihilism and vice. But I have no vices. And as for the absence of meaning … well, I already knew what that was like. No vice, no ambitions, no talents. My only talent seemed to be memory. Which, as you've seen, is both a blessing and a curse.
AMANDA. Are you done yet, Monsieur?
PRINCE. Almost. Because one day, into this fog which I could never leave, a woman came. And for three days where she passed, the fog dispersed and became light. A madwoman, I grant you, who rose at dusk and slept at dawn and whose nights were spent in an unending rush of incoherence interspersed with bits of opera and garbled Rumanian. She was passionate. And one evening she strangled herself with a gesture of her scarf after having spoken

entirely too long about the soul. It's in her memory that I let the village children mock me. They mocked her too … before she died and left me with nothing more than a memory which each day threatens to disappear. And as for the words "I love you," let me tell you this: She DID say "I LOVE YOU." She didn't say them in that order or together, but I am positive that in all the words she said to me there was an "I," there was a "love," there was a "you!" Mademoiselle, there is a price one pays for peace of mind, for a love that knows happiness and basks in the sun. There is also a price one pays for a different kind of love, a love that transfixes, that transforms. And that kind of love … that kind of love has little to do with happiness. *(A moment; he shouts suddenly:)* I don't love you, Mademoiselle! You are beautiful, more beautiful than even her! You are desirable, you are gay, you are tender; you are all that a man could ever want! You might even be right about everything … but I don't love you!
AMANDA. *(After a moment.)* Are you done now?
PRINCE. Now I am.
AMANDA. Good. Because I don't know who you think you were talking to. None of this matters to me. I couldn't care less. *(Amanda stands and crosses the café to the exit. Once there, she stops, collapses into tears and rushes off. The Prince, his tirade done, remains very stiff. He looks around him. He is alone. He goes to his table mechanically and, to the Headwaiter, who is approaching, he asks pitifully:)*
PRINCE. You know I loved her? Don't you? More than anything on earth? You knew that from the start, didn't you? You know I didn't … *not* love her.
HEADWAITER. *(Serves him champagne, obsequious.)* Monsieur! How can you ask such a question? Why … Monsieur worshiped, Monsieur adored! Sometimes even the staff commented upon it. No, no, it was one of the great loves! A love like that is unforgettable … even for those who never knew it. *(Turns toward the musicians.)* Music! *(The musicians vigorously play. The Prince collapses with his head in his hands. The curtain falls.)*

Scene 2

A grey and pink dawn. We're outside the Hotel Sainte-Anne-du-Pouldu as reconstructed in the park. Amanda, having cried herself to sleep, has slid to the ground in front of a stone bench. We hear gunshots in the distance. A beat later the Duchess and Hector enter, in old-fashioned hunting outfits, armed with long duck-guns. They are followed by the Butler carrying spare guns and empty game-bags.)

BUTLER. Your shot, Baron.
HECTOR. *(Fires out front; piqued.)* Missed. Damn.
BUTLER. Madame?
DUCHESS. *(Fires out front; delighted.)* Missed! Goody! It's always a great joy when I miss a bird! I do love so their flying and flapping and doing all those things birds do. Why do we shoot them, I wonder? *(Suddenly she sees Amanda.)* Heavens! Hector! Do you see that furl of white? Did you, against all reason and expectation, actually hit something?
HECTOR. I doubt it.
BUTLER. It's the lady, Madame. Your guest...?
DUCHESS. Is she damaged somehow?
BUTLER. No, Madame. She's asleep.
DUCHESS. *(Going to Amanda.)* Asleep? In the garden? I don't like that. So Biblical. So ripe for metaphor. Are those tears?
AMANDA. *(Wakes.)* Oh!
DUCHESS. My dear —
AMANDA. *(Stands.)* Please, Madame! Don't talk to me. I have to leave. Excuse me — !
DUCHESS. *(Makes signs to the Butler and Hector; they leave.)* Leave? Why?
AMANDA. Because I can't beat her.
DUCHESS. Who?
AMANDA. You know who I mean! I don't care about her, I want

you to understand that. I don't care about her, and I know, in my heart, I am stronger than she ever was. But she has more power than I.
DUCHESS. She may be powerful, but she has the practical disadvantage of being dead.
AMANDA. She didn't even let him touch her hand! And his hands are not rough! They're his hands, simple hands, hands made to take and to touch. If he only listened to them ... But he doesn't listen to his hands and he doesn't listen to me. He listens to her. And being dead, she cannot be contradicted!
DUCHESS. My dear. You're twenty years old, you're alive, and you're in love. That gives you more power than anything in the whole world. Look around you. Stop crying and look. The night is over. It's morning now. *(Indeed the light has changed around them, becoming a golden sunrise.)* The sun is just above the grass. It's almost dawn. Hope and flower petals open to the same rhythm: buds, leaves, the shutters of good people. And the smells, the first scents of the day: the warm, ripe earth, the dewy grass, the coffee that is homage to the day ... *(Indeed the Proprietor of the Hotel Sainte-Anne-du-Pouldu has opened his shutters and appeared at the door, yawning. Later, he will bring out the tables for the terrace.)* And the colors. They're at the purest in the morning — the truest pinks, the bluest blues, even the greens. Soon will come the bee and his buzz. The day is waiting. Léocadia was a creature of the night. Another world entirely. You are twenty years old; you are alive and you are in love. Stretch, sun yourself, laugh! All the powers of the morning are on your side. *(The Duchess goes off. The sun has become a blaze of gold. Amanda stretches out and laughs. She goes to the inn where the Proprietor has finished arranging the terrace.)*
AMANDA. Monsieur! Proprietor! *(Amanda taps on the table. He looks at her, goes to see if she has damaged the finish on the table, and then gives the table a hostile swiping of a rag.)* Is this the Hotel Sainte-Anne-du-Pouldu? *(The Proprietor points at the sign and nods.)* Are you mute?
PROPRIETOR. Oui.
AMANDA. Must be annoying to be mute.
PROPRIETOR. Nothing to speak of. You get used to it. Just like everything else around here.

AMANDA. What does one take for … muteness?
PROPRIETOR. I gargle.
AMANDA. Really?
PROPRIETOR. No, but I'm not really mute either. The concoction I make is made of tomatoes, red peppers, Tabasco, seltzer water and a secret ingredient.
AMANDA. And you gargle this concoction?
PROPRIETOR. Gargle, then swallow. The faster the better.
AMANDA. How often do you perform this ritual?
PROPRIETOR. Lunch, afternoon, dinner and bedtime. But I have to be careful. I have the liver of a man who's been dead for three weeks. Sometimes, I have my concoction in the morning too. It's actually pretty tasty.
AMANDA. I'm not thirsty.
PROPRIETOR. That's all right. Someone will drink it.
AMANDA. What about your liver?
PROPRIETOR. It's practically paté anyway. *(He goes into the inn and comes back with the bottles and the glasses.)* You're not from here are you?
AMANDA. No.
PROPRIETOR. Didn't you see the gate and the stone fence at the edge of the estate?
AMANDA. Well, you see, I —
PROPRIETOR. Don't worry. People roam in here by mistake all the time. They think it's a forest or a public park or … Germany. They even think this is a real café. I don't care, gets me a little extra business on the side. See, the owner of all this is a prince. And one summer this prince met a woman, spent three days with her in town, then she died. So you know what his family did? They had the whole town — every place he went with her — picked up and rebuilt right here. They say he's an "eccentric."
AMANDA. An "eccentric" is just someone you don't understand.
PROPRIETOR. Well, I don't understand him. This place is completely frozen in those three days that summer. When the grass gets brown in the fall, they have to paint it green, they have to paint the leaves on the trees and the flowers in the garden. Fools the eye, but don't get too close. They say it's so he can "remember." But I say: how can you remember something if you never leave it?

Personally, I think it was all a plot to relocate a legally zoned business district.
AMANDA. And this café is this where the prince and his young woman spent their last day.
PROPRIETOR. That's what they say.
AMANDA. You keep saying "say." Don't you remember?
PROPRIETOR. No. I wasn't there. This isn't my café. When the prince and the woman walked into the café that summer, the owners were an old couple. After the woman died and the prince's family arranged to move the town here, the couple told them they were ready to retire. So they sold the concern and hired me to manage it.
AMANDA. But if you weren't there the day the prince and the lady came in … how do you know what to do?
PROPRIETOR. I follow the script. Stick to the script, and everything goes fine. You wanna hear my lines?
AMANDA. Please.
PROPRIETOR. "Ah, Monsieur, why I just saw your taxi pull up! Mademoiselle looks so lovely in that scarf! Two lemonades! Why, of course! Coming right up!" *(Beat.)* That's it. "Blah-blah-blah-taxi, blah-blah-blah-scarf, blah-blah-blah-two-lemonades-coming up!" Between you and me, it's not a very good role. But as they say: "There are no small roles, just small actors with little to do who still have to hang around for the curtain call." So, sometimes, when I'm bored — and any actor will tell you this — I make things up. "Ah, Monsieur, why I just saw your taxi pull up! Do you know the driver is a hermaphrodite? Mademoiselle's scarf certainly looks lethal this morning. Lemonade? Sorry, all out of lemons, I can squeeze a couple of prunes, though!" He doesn't notice.
AMANDA. He doesn't?
PROPRIETOR. He says, "Oh, a hermaphrodite, that's nice." "Prunes; give her a double." He plays right along. I stopped using the script long ago. Improvisation is much more fun. I tell you something strange though: sometimes we stray so far from the original text … I'd swear the prince hadn't been there either.
AMANDA. … What?
PROPRIETOR. Really! I'd swear the man was never there. *(Beat.)* I should get back to work. Thanks for the drinks. That'll be three

francs fifty. *(He goes back to the inn.)*
AMANDA. Monsieur? Monsieur!
PROPRIETOR. *(Reappears on the threshold.)* What?
AMANDA. I like you very much!
PROPRIETOR. *(Worried.)* Why?
AMANDA. Because you have just given me a great gift.
PROPRIETOR. I have, huh? The drinks are still three francs fifty.
AMANDA. *(Gives him a coin.)* Here. Take this. And a tip.
PROPRIETOR. Thank you, Madame.
AMANDA. No. It is I who thanks you. *(At that moment the Prince enters, sleepy, his collar pulled up, shivering. The Proprietor does not see him. To Proprietor.)* Now go! Get out of here, quickly! *(The Proprietor exits inside the hotel.)*
PRINCE. *(Sees her suddenly.)* You're still here?
AMANDA. I am.
PRINCE. I ... apologize for my ... behavior last night.
AMANDA. Perish the thought. *(He shivers.)* Cold?
PRINCE. I always have a little chill in the morning.
AMANDA. Well, then, we must warm you up. Do you want to sit in the sun? *(The Prince advances; he looks at the inn.)*
PRINCE. No. I was cold that morning too. That's why we went inside the hotel.
AMANDA. I see. Well, what if we sat out here this morning, on the patio? Just for a change of pace.
PRINCE. *(Comes back to her.)* Well ... If you like. I'm usually just getting home now. *(Shivers.)* Mornings are cold, aren't they?
AMANDA. No, it's actually quite, quite hot. And there are bees. Hear them hum? Bees don't hum when it's cold.
PRINCE. Well, bees would know. *(Notes she is smiling.)* Why are you smiling?
AMANDA. Last night you frightened me. Now you don't. *(The Proprietor comes out.)*
PROPRIETOR. Say, where's the prin — ? *(Sees the Prince.)* Monsieur! "Why ... I didn't hear your taxi pull up."
AMANDA. He didn't come by taxi.
PROPRIETOR. Huh?
AMANDA. We'd like something to drink.
PROPRIETOR. Er ... "Two lemonades, coming right — "

AMANDA. No lemonade. Two cafés au lait.
PRINCE. Hot.
AMANDA. Very hot, Monsieur is cold.
PROPRIETOR. *(Confused.)* Two cafés au lait? Uh-huh. You know, I only said lemonade because the scrip — well, because it's usually lemonade, and — But if you want café au lait, I can make café au lait.
AMANDA. Large ones, with bread and butter.
PROPRIETOR. *(Getting angry.)* Large ones. Bread and butter. *(Hisses at Amanda.)* Scheming little vixen! You're trying to steal my part! *(He exits.)*
AMANDA. It doesn't bother you that we're going to have breakfast together?
PRINCE. No. No, it doesn't bother me. Why? Should it? *(Shoos away some bees.)* Damn.
AMANDA. What?
PRINCE. Bees.
AMANDA. Oh, don't chase them away.
PRINCE. They're bees. They sting. You want to watch them bite me?
AMANDA. They won't bite. I promise.
PRINCE. You seem to like the morning. You seem very "at home" in the sun.
AMANDA. And I am very happy to receive you at my home with my bees and under my sun.
PRINCE. *(Looks at her and murmurs.)* Now you're starting to frighten me.
AMANDA. Really?
PRINCE. You're like some demonic wood nymph. Crafty, pink and on the prowl. *(The Proprietor brings coffee and milk in blue cups, a heap of bread with butter.)*
PROPRIETOR. Two cafés au lait.
AMANDA. Ah! Many thanks.
PROPRIETOR. Shall I … bring the lemonade also?
AMANDA. No!
PROPRIETOR. No?
AMANDA. No.
PRINCE. Do as the lady says.

PROPRIETOR. Uh-huh. Well. All right. *(Hisses.)* Mademoiselle! You have upstaged me! *(He storms off.)*
PRINCE. Are you really going to eat all that?
AMANDA. I am, and don't try to change my mind. Anything you might do is doomed to failure. This morning, I'm not ashamed of my appetite. This morning, I am starving.
PRINCE. ... Who are you?
AMANDA. Just a young girl in a white dress, buttering her bread in the sun.
PRINCE. Didn't I meet you the other night in the park near the statue?
AMANDA. Mmm. I asked you the way to the sea. The next day we met again at the chateau of your aunt and then we rented a boat and rowed up the river. Yesterday evening, after a long silent afternoon basking in the sun, we went to the Blue Danube. The café with the gypsies who sang, "We waltzed and waltzed ... "
PRINCE and AMANDA. "But then you somehow slipped away ... "
AMANDA. But it's morning now. And we're eating breakfast together at this little hotel you mentioned last night. It's nice in the sun at your little hotel.
PRINCE. *(Cries suddenly, anguished.)* But it's the last day!
AMANDA. *(Calmly.)* "Last?" Oh, no, no. It's the third. The third day. And it's only just begun.
PRINCE. But what about tonight?
AMANDA. Well, darling, tonight, we'll do whatever you like.
PRINCE. And tomorrow?
AMANDA. That will be the fourth day. And we'll be here, together, like we are this morning. *(The Prince shivers; Amanda takes his arm.)*
PRINCE. I'm cold, let's go in.
AMANDA. No.
PRINCE. What means this "no?"
AMANDA. It means let's stay out in the sun.
PRINCE. I don't want to.
AMANDA. Don't you love me?
PRINCE. *(Cries.)* I do not!
AMANDA. *(Gently.)* Oh, you love me. If you didn't love me, you

wouldn't yell so loud. Stop struggling. You've just woken up. It was all a bad dream. And the night is gone and the morning has come to save the day. Look. Look closely at all the real things around us, flowers one can smell, grass one can hold in one's hands. *(She is facing him. She suddenly says in a breath:)* Place your hands on me. I am going to show you how everything is going to be all right.
PRINCE. No.
AMANDA. Why not?
PRINCE. I'm afraid.
AMANDA. There's no reason. Your hands are strong hands. Listen to them. They're saying: "Let the memory go." And that's good. Put your two hands on me, please.
PRINCE. If I touch you, I'll love you. And I don't want to touch you.
AMANDA. Yesterday you were "The Prince" — now you're a fish struggling against the current, against the whole force of the world rushing down on you. *(Sound of a shotgun blast off. Then a mournful cry echoes through the park, followed by the flutter of a hundred wings.)*
PRINCE. *(Sighs in spite of himself.)* Léocadia …
AMANDA. *(Very softly.)* Love? Put your hands on my hips. *(A silence. The Prince suddenly puts his hands around her and doesn't move anymore. She has closed her eyes, she murmurs:)* You're not saying anything. It's me who is afraid now.
PRINCE. *(Gazes at her.)* How simple. How easy. How real. *(He kisses her suddenly. A long kiss, a long embrace. Then the walls of the little inn open. Amanda and the Prince exit inside the inn, hand in hand. Then the walls close in on them. Beat. Another gunshot and a large, dead bird crashes to the stage floor. The Duchess and Hector enter, guns lowered. Behind them is the Butler.)*
DUCHESS. It was you, I tell you! Your shot! You got it, Hector!
HECTOR. It couldn't have been me! You say yourself I'm such a bad shot, I never hit anything!
DUCHESS. You're such a bad shot the odds were you'd have to hit something someday!
HECTOR. But I don't even aim anymore! You aimed! I saw you! I'd swear to the death!
DUCHESS. Swear, die, you're still the culprit. Admit it, Hector, you shot a heron!

BUTLER. It wasn't a heron, Madame. Nor a flamingo. It was an extravagant bird one doesn't often see in the countryside. Long feathers, so long they catch on everything, feet too high, doesn't know how to walk or perch. And a plumage you can see at five hundred paces. Couldn't miss if you tried. And that call, that cry. When you fired, Madame —
HECTOR. You see, even he says you shot it!
DUCHESS. All right, so it was me! I came, I saw, I shot the bird! Happy? Theophilus, you may return to the house. And take the creature with you.
BUTLER. But, Madame, what do I do with it? You can't even eat it.
DUCHESS. Bury it.
BUTLER. Bury it?
DUCHESS. Under my rose bushes. *(The Butler takes the bird, bows and leaves. A silence. The Duchess and Hector sit down side by side on the bench; they stare off a beat. Abruptly:)* What are you thinking about, Hector?
HECTOR. *(Jumps.)* Nothing. Everything. I was thinking about ...
DUCHESS. Me too. Poor Léocadia! We've just killed her a second time. In his memory. But it was necessary. How else save our little Albert? And if it is the young Amandas of the world who will save the little Alberts, well, vive le young Amandas! But as useless, frivolous and downright unpleasant as that awful Léocadia was ... I shall miss her. I shall shed a tear for her, my dear. If just a little one.
HECTOR. *(Moved.)* Don't cry, old girl.
DUCHESS. *(Eyes him scornfully, severely.)* I wasn't talking to you, Hector. *(She points at the sky.)* I was talking to Gaston. *(Sound of birds chirping. Lights fade to black.)*

End of Play

PROPERTY LIST

Large dead bird
Cardboard suitcase (AMANDA)
Lorgnette (DUCHESS)
Green gloves (AMANDA)
Table with silver, cakes and fruit (BUTLER)
Tangerine (AMANDA)
Monocle (HECTOR)
Bicycle (PRINCE)
Chair (DUCHESS)
Blindfold (HEADWAITER)
File (BUTLER)
Cards (MARIA)
Violin, bow (FLAGEL)
Clarinet (PESHKE)
Cigarette, newspaper, paper and pen (HEADWAITER)
Violin case with bottle of Pernod (BELA)
Bucket of ice, glasses (HEADWAITER)
Bottle of champagne, champagne bucket (HEADWAITER)
Cloak (HEADWAITER)
Duck guns (DUCHESS, HECTOR)
Guns, game bags (BUTLER)
Tables, chairs, rag (PROPRIETOR)
Bottles, glasses (PROPRIETOR)
Coin (AMANDA)
Two blue cups of coffee, bread and butter (PROPRIETOR)

SOUND EFFECTS

Music
Birds chirping
Motor turning over
Bicycle bell
Waltz
Gypsy music
Violin music
Lively music
Gunshots
Mournful cry, flutter of wings

Where Went The Waltz
"TO FOOL THE EYE"

Music by Andrew Cooke
Lyrics by Jeffrey Hatcher

Copyright 2000

NEW PLAYS

★ **THE CREDEAUX CANVAS by Keith Bunin.** A forged painting leads to tragedy among friends. "There is that moment between adolescence and middle age when being disaffected looks attractive. Witness the enduring appeal of Prince Hamlet, Jake Barnes and James Dean, on the stage, page and screen. Or, more immediately, take a look at the lithe young things in THE CREDEAUX CANVAS..." –*NY Times.* "THE CREDEAUX CANVAS is the third recent play about painters...it turned out to be the best of the lot, better even than most plays about non-painters." –*NY Magazine.* [2M, 2W] ISBN: 0-8222-1838-0

★ **THE DIARY OF ANNE FRANK by Frances Goodrich and Albert Hackett, newly adapted by Wendy Kesselman.** A transcendently powerful new adaptation in which Anne Frank emerges from history a living, lyrical, intensely gifted young girl. "Undeniably moving. It shatters the heart. The evening never lets us forget the inhuman darkness waiting to claim its incandescently human heroine." –*NY Times.* "A sensitive, stirring and thoroughly engaging new adaptation." –*NY Newsday.* "A powerful new version that moves the audience to gasps, then tears." –*A.P.* "One of the year's ten best." –*Time Magazine.* [5M, 5W, 3 extras] ISBN: 0-8222-1718-X

★ **THE BOOK OF LIZ by David Sedaris and Amy Sedaris.** Sister Elizabeth Donderstock makes the cheese balls that support her religious community, but feeling unappreciated among the Squeamish, she decides to try her luck in the outside world. "...[a] delightfully off-key, off-color hymn to clichés we all live by, whether we know it or not." –*NY Times.* "Good-natured, goofy and frequently hilarious..." –*NY Newsday.* "...[THE BOOK OF LIZ] may well be the world's first Amish picaresque...hilarious..." –*Village Voice.* [2M, 2W (doubling, flexible casting to 8M, 7W)] ISBN: 0-8222-1827-5

★ **JAR THE FLOOR by Cheryl L. West.** A quartet of black women spanning four generations makes up this hilarious and heartwarming dramatic comedy. "...a moving and hilarious account of a black family sparring in a Chicago suburb..." –*NY Magazine.* "...heart-to-heart confrontations and surprising revelations...first-rate..." –*NY Daily News.* "...unpretentious good feelings...bubble through West's loving and humorous play..." –*Star-Ledger.* "...one of the wisest plays I've seen in ages...[from] a master playwright." –*USA Today.* [5W] ISBN: 0-8222-1809-7

★ **THIEF RIVER by Lee Blessing.** Love between two men over decades is explored in this incisive portrait of coming to terms with who you are. "Mr. Blessing unspools the plot ingeniously, skipping back and forth in time as the details require...an absorbing evening." –*NY Times.* "...wistful and sweet-spirited..." –*Variety.* [6M] ISBN: 0-8222-1839-9

★ **THE BEGINNING OF AUGUST by Tom Donaghy.** When Jackie's wife abruptly and mysteriously leaves him and their infant daughter, a pungently comic reevaluation of suburban life ensues. "Donaghy holds a cracked mirror up to the contemporary American family, anatomizing its frailties and miscommunications in fractured language that can be both funny and poignant." –*The Philadelphia Inquirer.* "...[A] sharp, eccentric new comedy. Pungently funny...fresh and precise..." –*LA Times.* [3M, 2W] ISBN: 0-8222-1786-4

★ **OUTSTANDING MEN'S MONOLOGUES 2001–2002 and OUTSTANDING WOMEN'S MONOLOGUES 2001–2002 edited by Craig Pospisil.** Drawn exclusively from Dramatists Play Service publications, these collections for actors feature over fifty monologues each and include an enormous range of voices, subject matter and characters. MEN'S ISBN: 0-8222-1821-6 WOMEN'S ISBN: 0-8222-1822-4

DRAMATISTS PLAY SERVICE, INC.
440 Park Avenue South, New York, NY 10016 212-683-8960 Fax 212-213-1539
postmaster@dramatists.com www.dramatists.com

NEW PLAYS

★ **A LESSON BEFORE DYING** by Romulus Linney, based on the novel by Ernest J. Gaines. An innocent young man is condemned to death in backwoods Louisiana and must learn to die with dignity. "The story's wrenching power lies not in its outrage but in the almost inexplicable grace the characters must muster as their only resistance to being treated like lesser beings." *–The New Yorker.* "Irresistable momentum and a cathartic explosion…a powerful inevitability." *–NY Times.* [5M, 2W] ISBN: 0-8222-1785-6

★ **BOOM TOWN** by Jeff Daniels. A searing drama mixing small-town love, politics and the consequences of betrayal. "…a brutally honest, contemporary foray into classic themes, exploring what moves people to lie, cheat, love and dream. By BOOM TOWN's climactic end there are no secrets, only bare truth." *–Oakland Press.* "…some of the most electrifying writing Daniels has ever done…" *–Ann Arbor News.* [2M, 1W] ISBN: 0-8222-1760-0

★ **INCORRUPTIBLE** by Michael Hollinger. When a motley order of medieval monks learns their patron saint no longer works miracles, a larcenous, one-eyed minstrel shows them an outrageous new way to pay old debts. "A lightning-fast farce, rich in both verbal and physical humor." *–American Theatre.* "Everything fits snugly in this funny, endearing black comedy…an artful blend of the mock-formal and the anachronistically breezy…A piece of remarkably dexterous craftsmanship." *–Philadelphia Inquirer.* "A farcical romp, scintillating and irreverent." *–Philadelphia Weekly.* [5M, 3W] ISBN: 0-8222-1787-2

★ **CELLINI** by John Patrick Shanley. Chronicles the life of the original "Renaissance Man," Benvenuto Cellini, the sixteenth-century Italian sculptor and man-about-town. Adapted from the autobiography of Benvenuto Cellini, translated by J. Addington Symonds. "[Shanley] has created a convincing Cellini, not neglecting his dark side, and a trim, vigorous, fast-moving show." *–BackStage.* "Very entertaining…With brave purpose, the narrative undermines chronology before untangling it…touching and funny…" *–NY Times.* [7M, 2W (doubling)] ISBN: 0-8222-1808-9

★ **PRAYING FOR RAIN** by Robert Vaughan. Examines a burst of fatal violence and its aftermath in a suburban high school. "Thought provoking and compelling." *–Denver Post.* "Vaughan's powerful drama offers hope and possibilities." *–Theatre.com.* "[The play] doesn't put forth compact, tidy answers to the problem of youth violence. What it does offer is a compelling exploration of the forces that influence an individual's choices, and of the proverbial lifelines—be they familial, communal, religious or political—that tragically slacken when society gives in to apathy, fear and self-doubt…" *–Westword.*"…a symphony of anger…" *–Gazette Telegraph.* [4M, 3W] ISBN: 0-8222-1807-0

★ **GOD'S MAN IN TEXAS** by David Rambo. When a young pastor takes over one of the most prestigious Baptist churches from a rip-roaring old preacher-entrepreneur, all hell breaks loose. "…the pick of the litter of all the works at the Humana Festival…" *–Providence Journal.* "…a wealth of both drama and comedy in the struggle for power…" *–LA Times.* "…the first act is so funny…deepens in the second act into a sobering portrait of fear, hope and self-delusion…" *–Columbus Dispatch.* [3M] ISBN: 0-8222-1801-1

★ **JESUS HOPPED THE 'A' TRAIN** by Stephen Adly Guirgis. A probing, intense portrait of lives behind bars at Rikers Island. "…fire-breathing…whenever it appears that JESUS is settling into familiar territory, it slides right beneath expectations into another, fresher direction. It has the courage of its intellectual restlessness…[JESUS HOPPED THE 'A' TRAIN] has been written in flame." *–NY Times.* [4M, 1W] ISBN: 0-8222-1799-6

DRAMATISTS PLAY SERVICE, INC.
440 Park Avenue South, New York, NY 10016 212-683-8960 Fax 212-213-1539
postmaster@dramatists.com www.dramatists.com

NEW PLAYS

★ **THE CIDER HOUSE RULES, PARTS 1 & 2 by Peter Parnell**, adapted from the novel by John Irving. Spanning eight decades of American life, this adaptation from the Irving novel tells the story of Dr. Wilbur Larch, founder of the St. Cloud's, Maine orphanage and hospital, and of the complex father-son relationship he develops with the young orphan Homer Wells. "...luxurious digressions, confident pacing...an enterprise of scope and vigor..." –*NY Times*. "...The fact that I can't wait to see Part 2 only begins to suggest just how good it is..." –*NY Daily News*. "...engrossing...an odyssey that has only one major shortcoming: It comes to an end." –*Seattle Times*. "...outstanding...captures the humor, the humility...of Irving's 588-page novel..." –*Seattle Post-Intelligencer*. [9M, 10W, doubling, flexible casting] PART 1 ISBN: 0-8222-1725-2 PART 2 ISBN: 0-8222-1726-0

★ **TEN UNKNOWNS by Jon Robin Baitz**. An iconoclastic American painter in his seventies has his life turned upside down by an art dealer and his ex-boyfriend. "...breadth and complexity...a sweet and delicate harmony rises from the four cast members...Mr. Baitz is without peer among his contemporaries in creating dialogue that spontaneously conveys a character's social context and moral limitations..." –*NY Times*. "...darkly funny, brilliantly desperate comedy...TEN UNKNOWNS vibrates with vital voices." –*NY Post*. [3M, 1W] ISBN: 0-8222-1826-7

★ **BOOK OF DAYS by Lanford Wilson**. A small-town actress playing St. Joan struggles to expose a murder. "...[Wilson's] best work since *Fifth of July*...An intriguing, prismatic and thoroughly engrossing depiction of contemporary small-town life with a murder mystery at its core...a splendid evening of theater..." –*Variety*. "...fascinating...a densely populated, unpredictable little world." –*St. Louis Post-Dispatch*. [6M, 5W] ISBN: 0-8222-1767-8

★ **THE SYRINGA TREE by Pamela Gien**. Winner of the 2001 Obie Award. A breathtakingly beautiful tale of growing up white in apartheid South Africa. "Instantly engaging, exotic, complex, deeply shocking...a thoroughly persuasive transport to a time and a place...stun[s] with the power of a gut punch..." –*NY Times*. "Astonishing...affecting ...[with] a dramatic and heartbreaking conclusion...A deceptive sweet simplicity haunts THE SYRINGA TREE..." –*A.P.* [1W (or flexible cast)] ISBN: 0-8222-1792-9

★ **COYOTE ON A FENCE by Bruce Graham**. An emotionally riveting look at capital punishment. "The language is as precise as it is profane, provoking both troubling thought and the occasional cheerful laugh...will change you a little before it lets go of you." –*Cincinnati CityBeat*. "...excellent theater in every way..." –*Philadelphia City Paper*. [3M, 1W] ISBN: 0-8222-1738-4

★ **THE PLAY ABOUT THE BABY by Edward Albee**. Concerns a young couple who have just had a baby and the strange turn of events that transpire when they are visited by an older man and woman. "An invaluable self-portrait of sorts from one of the few genuinely great living American dramatists...rockets into that special corner of theater heaven where words shoot off like fireworks into dazzling patterns and hues." –*NY Times*. "An exhilarating, wicked...emotional terrorism." –*NY Newsday*. [2M, 2W] ISBN: 0-8222-1814-3

★ **FORCE CONTINUUM by Kia Corthron**. Tensions among black and white police officers and the neighborhoods they serve form the backdrop of this discomfiting look at life in the inner city. "The creator of this intense...new play is a singular voice among American playwrights...exceptionally eloquent..." –*NY Times*. "...a rich subject and a wise attitude." –*NY Post*. [6M, 2W, 1 boy] ISBN: 0-8222-1817-8

DRAMATISTS PLAY SERVICE, INC.
440 Park Avenue South, New York, NY 10016 212-683-8960 Fax 212-213-1539
postmaster@dramatists.com www.dramatists.com